IS HE?

GREGORY GATEFIELD

IS HE?

GREGORY GATEFIELD

Cover design and art by J. S. Burris

Table of Contents

Preface....................1

Introduction....................4

A Timeline of the End of Days....................9

The Countdown to the End....................15

Chapter 1: The Millenial Day Theory....................17

Chapter 2: Signs of the Times....................23

Chapter 3: The Chosen Generation....................27

Chapter 4 - The Holy Land....................35

The Apocalypse....................39

Chapter 5: The Rapture....................40

Chapter 6: The Tribulation....................45

Chapter 7: The Antichrist is not Satan....................52

Chapter 8: The False Prophet....................55

Chapter 9: Debunking the "Unholy Trinity"....................57

The Beast....................62

Chapter 10: The Beast's Traits....................64

Chapter 11: The Mark of the Beast....................68

Chapter 12: The Upside-Down..87

Chapter 13: The Beast's Traits Revisited..........................97

The Deceiver and the Dictator...107

Chapter 14: The Conspicuous Warning...........................108

Chapter 15: The Beast in Lamb's Clothing.....................114

Chapter 16: The Beast Reveals Himself...........................129

If it Happens...147

Chapter 17: The Rapture Envisioned...............................150

Chapter 18 - The Internet Apocalypse.............................157

Chapter 19 - What Now?..183

Epilogue..185

Bonus Chapter: The Curious Case of the Imaginary I.D. 187

Preface

Since the beginnings of recorded human history, it seems mankind has been obsessed with the end of the world. That obsession continues today, and for many it has become an all-encompassing passion. We live in the age of conspiracy theories, and no other theories, conspiracy or otherwise, carry such colossal importance as do the theories on the apocalypse.

The end of the world appears in mythology and across several religions. One could write volumes on this subject, a thorough and exhaustive encyclopedia of all the pained thoughts and theories of philosophers, scholars, prophets, religious clerics, preachers, and inquisitive laymen alike. I will not be writing that book. I won't pretend to grapple with such complex, varied scholarly traditions. I simply don't have the time. Because the end of the world may be getting very close. I've been told that since I was a kid. I'm still being told that today.

America is a diverse nation, our population a potpourri of different cultures, ethnicities, and religions. But from the founding of America until this day nearly 250 years later, one religion has dominated the American culture at large - Christianity. As such, everyday words in our American culture come straight from the Bible. The faithful and agnostic alike know these words and their general meanings and imagery. When Ben Affleck stars in a movie about an asteroid destroying the earth, it is of course given the biblical title Armageddon. We get the reference even if we've never walked into a church. In that same manner, this book will shamelessly tackle the end of days through the narrow lens of modern evangelical Christianity. That is what I know, and what I know scares the hell out of me.

PREFACE

I also know one more word: Antichrist. I heard that word a lot in the 80's, the 90's, the zeros, the two thousand teens, and now. Most recently, I see it in memes on social media sites. But I mostly heard it at church, a very southern baptist church. I heard it in Sunday school, in Sunday morning sermons, in Sunday evening sermons, at Wednesday evening bible study, at church camp, and at home. I heard it a lot at home.

Yes, many of us search for our destinies. It seems my destiny may have always been to try to spot the ultimate wolf in sheep's clothing, or in this case the Beast in Lamb's clothing. Time will tell. I do not know the exact day or hour of the end of the world or the return of Jesus. No man does. But the Bible gives us clues, and the evidence is substantial. We are given those clues so we can be prepared. The Antichrist may very well be walking amongst us. You may have seen him on tv, in magazines, in person, or simply in the news, a man of unimaginable fame and fortune and stature and influence and power. But is it really him? Does he even know it is him? Is he hiding in plain sight? Is he the one to usher in the end of days and fool the Church? Is he really the Beast in the flesh? Is he?

In the interest of full disclosure, I was not just a church kid. I am a born-again Christian to this day. I believe in the grace of God the Father through the sacrifice of his Son, Jesus Christ. It is that faith that I pray guides me in the writing of this book.

In 1997, I saw "The Devil's Advocate", a film fittingly set in the rural American South. I saw Keanu Reeves play a morally-conflicted lawyer who unknowingly works for and represents the Devil himself (the masterful Al Pacino). Over twenty-five years later, this forgotten film has resurfaced in my mind and life in unimaginable ways. In all my years studying the prophets, the

Scriptures, the Book of Revelation, and our world at large, it never, ever occurred to me that the Antichrist would be lawyered up. But that's how life works sometimes. You envision things one way when they are hypothetical. But when things become real and materialize slowly before you, it's the little details, both humorous and maddening, that begin to take shape. This little detail of the Antichrist being surrounded by lawyers never made sense until now.

To fulfill his destiny as the Beast of Revelation, it is essential for him to squash and conceal any educated writings and speculation as to his identity. In the literary world, the issues of libel and defamation come to mind. How could one ever reach the masses, other than the factually-challenged misinformation gutters known as social media and message boards? How could one speculate about the Antichrist's specific identity and ever hope to get published? How indeed could one accomplish this if the Antichrist was ready to sue and ruin any and all who challenge him? As such, it now makes perfect sense that if the Beast were with us now, just before his ascent to full world dominion, he would likely be the most litigious man in the world, synonymous with lawsuits and court filings and attorneys. He would surely be ready. If you are reading this book, a brave publisher has taken the chance, and I am eternally grateful.

Introduction

The question before you today is a most unusual and pressing one. It is not an allegation or accusation. It is simply a question - a question of great consequence and urgency. No matter how I ask "Is He?", it is the same question. Is the red-hatted politician the future Beast of Revelation? Is the criminally-convicted bombastic billionaire the biblical Man of Lawlessness? Is the most famous man on earth the prophesied Antichrist?

To be sure, it is a loaded, difficult question. The task before you today, however, is simple. You do not need to come to a decision or render any sort of verdict. Your only task is to read the evidence - read and think critically with an open mind. That's it, simply consider the evidence.

Over the coming chapters, that is exactly what you will encounter - evidence. There is a lot of it. These pages will explore and analyze everything the Bible tells us about the prophesied Beast - his personality, his physical qualities, his actions, his mark and his agenda. At the same time, this book will explore and analyze the same attributes of the red-hatted politician. Do his personality, physical qualities, actions, trademark and agenda match up to those of the prophesied Antichrist?

INTRODUCTION

In order to tell the full story, this book must ask and explore other questions. There must be context. Just like in a real criminal case, it is not enough to simply discuss the suspect. There is so much more to it than that. A prosecutor must discuss the timeframe and the setting - the scene of the crime. A prosecutor must show a suspect's opportunity and motive. A prosecutor must establish any accomplices and any smoking gun evidence that links all the evidence together. That is exactly what this book will seek to do. While the question this book poses is not an actual criminal case, the analogy nevertheless applies.

Section 1: The timeframe of the Antichrist's ascension to a worldwide reign is just before the apocalyptic end of the world. So the first question this book must tackle is about just that, the end of the world.

Are the biblical signs of the end of the world and return of Jesus being fulfilled today? Is that time almost upon us?

If it is not, then the red-hatted politician cannot be the Beast, period. But if the end is indeed near, then it means the Antichrist is already alive on earth today. It is that simple.

As such, this book's first section will tackle the biblical prophecies and signs of the apocalypse. This first section is a necessary building block to give context to the larger picture.

Section 2: The setting of the Beast's reign is on a throne of power during the Great Tribulation, a time of hell on earth detailed in the prophetic Book of Revelation. In the second section of this book, the Tribulation will be explored, as will the Rapture - the mysterious happening that ends all normalcy on earth and kick-starts the Tribulation. This second section will also lay key groundwork about the Antichrist as understood from Scripture, dispelling the myth that the Beast is Satan in the flesh. Lastly, the Beast's powerful accomplice, the "false prophet" or enabler, will be introduced. This second section is also a necessary building block to give context to the larger picture.

Section 3: After establishing the prerequisite context, a prosecutor can then introduce detailed evidence about a suspect. That is what the shocking third section of this book is all about. Everything the Bible tells us about the Beast will be explored. Then, our subject will be analyzed. Are the traits the same? Do they have the same mark or trademark? Do they share the same specific physical description? Do not put this book aside until you have read this third section fully. It contains multiple explosive bombshells that will literally turn your thinking upside-down.

Section 4: As mentioned, a prosecutor must also establish the motive and opportunity of a suspect, the methods and means he employs. The fourth section of this book will tackle these specific issues. The Bible suggests that the Antichrist will deceive mankind in his ascent to power. Even some devout Christians will be fooled. Moreover, the Beast will become a global dictator who demands absolute loyalty. Has the red-hatted politician fooled Christians? Is he now in a position of power and influence to become an authoritative dictator? Does he have a motive to do so?

Section 5: Lastly, a good prosecutor must tie all the pieces of a crime together. The evidence must be fully connected to show how the crime was committed by the suspect at the crime scene. The role of any accomplices must be established.

The fifth and final section of this book is the toughest for this author to write. It is mostly forward-looking and in the future. Unlike the above analogy of a courtroom, in this case the crime has not been committed, yet. The world is not being ruled by the Antichrist, yet. Our subject cannot be guilty, yet. Again, this book is a question and not an accusation.

As such, the final section of this book is a shocking hypothetical. It meticulously pieces together several biblical prophecies that can only now be rationally explained in the 21st century. To be clear, these prophecies never made any logical sense until now. If the end of the world is near, how does the apocalypse begin? How could the Beast rise to worldwide power? How does the powerful "false prophet" aid and abet the Beast, and just who could this enabler be? The last chapter of this book is a sobering, thought-provoking glimpse at just how fragile our 21st century technology might really be. Our advanced world of electricity, satellites, and the internet could literally go dark in the blink of an eye. If the unthinkable happens, who is best positioned to turn the lights back on and fill the power void? Who will become the Beast's closest ally and help him do it all?

Above all else, this book seeks to inspire thought and ask questions. We live in an era of "doing our own research." I've done my research and analyzed the world around me. As you are about to see, that research and analysis is extensive and exhaustive. This book was written over the course of two years, with world events frequently requiring critical updates. Those updates have been noted and inserted into the original chapters as warranted. The reader is again encouraged to think critically with an open mind and consider the merits of what follows. The reader is free to reach his/her own conclusions. If nothing else, I trust this book will be a good education and insight into a worldview different from your own. And if anything you read or hear surfaces in the future (like an eerie "Simpsons" prediction), I trust you keep this book for future reference.

To best appreciate and comprehend this book, it is important to first understand words and terms and concepts mentioned frequently. I grew up attending an evangelical Christian church, so these words and events and concepts have been in my vernacular since childhood. Others with this background may likewise be familiar with all of these. Nevertheless, this is a book for all people, so a primer seems prerequisite. In the remainder of this introduction, I will lay out a timeline of "the end of days", "the apocalypse", or "the return of Jesus" as best understood from Scripture. I will also define certain terms and ideas as necessary, again with the expectation that not all who stumble upon this book will have the same familiarity that us church kids do.

A Timeline of the End of Days

The "end of the world" as we know it, according to Scripture, is not just a lightning-strike moment in time. It is not the earth exploding or imploding or all of humanity dying or vanishing at once. Rather, the Biblical "end of the world" will occur through a sequence of events. Much of this is spelled out clearly in the Bible. Some of it is much murkier and open to interpretation.

A TIMELINE OF THE END OF DAYS

Different branches of Christianity espouse different beliefs in this area. I write what I know and believe. Take it or leave it. What I am presenting is what a large number of evangelical Christians believe, what many an evangelical preacher has delivered in sermons for decades. It is rooted in Scripture, but again the scriptures can be vague or murky at times. Without further ado, the timeline of the end of days:

1. Life as normal/ current life - ok, this one is my term. I consider it the world we have all known and live in today (at least until the time of publishing). More specifically, this is the time after the death and resurrection of Christ roughly 2000 years ago up through at least 2024 AD. In layman's terms, it means that none of the final apocalyptic events prophesied in the Bible have begun yet. There may be clues and signs out there that the return of Jesus is near, but nothing definitive has occurred that thrusts us into the absolute end times. Think of now as before the countdown for a space launch. Some people are warning that a launch could happen soon. Some may even say it is very, very soon, that they see the rocket rolled out onto the launching pad. But the countdown clock has not been definitively started. That is where we are in 2024, the official countdown clock has not begun.

2. Rapture - The first event to keep an eye out for is the Rapture. This event is detailed in the Bible, specifically in 2 Thessalonians 2:7-8 and 1 Corinthians 15:52. The Rapture is a reaping of souls from the earth, caught up in the air to meet the Lord Jesus. It is not the return or second coming of Jesus to the earth, though for believers in Christ, it might as well be. Many evangelicals believe that faithful

believers in Christ will be spared from the terrible last days and years on the earth before the return of Jesus. Theoretically, thousands or millions of people worldwide could vanish from the earth in an instant, joining Jesus in the air and being whisked away to heaven. It would undoubtedly be a cataclysmic, momentous event, a happening of epic proportions. Millions of evangelical Christians today are consciously or subconsciously keeping an eye out for this event. The Rapture would seemingly begin the official countdown to the end. No man will know the day or hour of the return of Jesus or indeed of the Rapture, but we may know the figurative season. The Rapture is detailed and considered in great length later in this book.

3. Tribulation - After the Rapture, the earth will descend into a time of great peril and chaos and plagues and hardships. This is detailed in the book of Revelation. Many believe that the period of time between the Rapture and the return of Jesus is roughly seven years. The seven year period is broken into halves, or two periods of 3.5 years each. The terrible but less harsh first half of this time period is the first half of the full Tribulation. It is prudent to note that the Bible is not super clear on everything about the Tribulation. There are numerous interpretations and schools of thought, especially involving the timing or length. Some believe it is only 3.5 years long in total. While I may presuppose a seven-year Tribulation at times, again Scripture can be vague and symbolic. Ultimately, this book is designed to provoke thought and raise questions, not give definitive answers.

4. Great Tribulation - Assuming a seven-year Tribulation, the

second half (3.5 years) before Jesus returns is often called the Great Tribulation. At the start of this time period, the Beast will emerge to rule over the earth. He is depicted as being healed from a mortal head wound. The Beast is also referred to elsewhere in the Bible as the Man of Lawlessness or the Antichrist. I will use all three terms interchangeably. The Beast will have an accomplice or sidekick who performs great wonders. Scripture refers to this man as the second beast or false prophet.

5. The Second Coming of Jesus Christ - Per Scripture and detailed late in the Book of Revelation, Jesus will return to earth at the end of the Great Tribulation. No man will know the day or the hour of this occurrence.

6. The Battle of Armageddon - This occurs immediately after the return of Jesus to earth. Jesus returns with the "armies of heaven" (Mark 14:62). It is detailed in Revelation 19 how Jesus defeats the forces and armies on earth that do battle for the Beast, the Antichrist. The two beasts (the Antichrist and the false prophet) are thrown into the lake of fire.

7. The Millennial Kingdom - After the Battle of Armageddon, Satan will be bound up and thrown into a bottomless pit for 1,000 years (Revelation 20:1-3). Jesus will rule on earth for this 1,000 years on a throne in Jerusalem. It will be a time of peace and prosperity.

8. The final battle, final judgment, and creation of a new heaven and new earth - The final chapters of Revelation suggest that after the millennial reign of Christ on earth,

> Satan will be released but quickly defeated. At that time, God will issue a final judgment of individuals from his great white throne, and a new heaven and new earth of paradise will be created for all faithful believers for eternity.

This book is a thoughtful look at whether the great Beast, the Antichrist, is on the scene today, closer than ever to beginning his full worldwide authoritarian reign. As such, the events after the return of Jesus and defeat of the Beast will not be explored with any depth.

Before continuing on, it seems prudent to define a few terms. The term ***evangelical Christian***, or simply ***evangelicals***, is often heard in mainstream media, specifically as a voting bloc or focus group in elections. I will use this term often. I am one. Evangelicals are Christians who believe (or are taught) it is their duty to spread their faith, to evangelize, to share the good news of Jesus' amazing, saving grace. They generally stress that the Bible is the Word of God and that personal conversion through accepting Jesus is the key to eternal life. Examples of evangelical denominations of Christianity include most Protestant churches, such as Southern Baptist, Church of God, Methodist, Pentecostal, and many non-denominational churches.

It is common among many evangelicals to believe that we are living in the ***end times***, which I will define as the timeline listed above beginning with the Rapture. Throughout this book, I will use the terms ***end times*** or ***end of days*** or ***apocalypse*** almost interchangeably, always a reference to the events to come, whether it be the Rapture, the Great Tribulation, the final battle of Armageddon, etc. Evangelicals often use the phrase '***a sign of the***

times.' This refers to signs and clues and events that they believe indicate we are living near the end times and that Jesus is soon to return. You may have heard some people say that the war in Israel is a "sign of the times." This is what they mean.

The term ***apocalypse*** is found throughout pop culture. People think of it as either the end of the world, or some horrible, life-altering event or series of events that changes the earth forever. One generally associates the apocalypse with death and suffering for the multitudes. Countless science fiction books and movies and television shows center around the apocalypse or a post-apocalyptic scenario. This pretty much jives with how I will use the term as well. Specifically, I will refer to the apocalypse as a familiar term for life on earth after the Rapture, for life on earth during the Great Tribulation, for life on earth when the return of Jesus is very near. I will not use the word apocalypse to refer to zombies.

A similar phrase used by evangelicals is '***new world order***.' The phrase is often used generically in the news to signal geopolitical changes (such as the collapse of the Soviet Union) or changing alliances or any sort of economic or political upheaval on a global scale. In pop culture, the term was memorably adopted in the entertainment arena of professional wrestling. In the late 1990's (and borrowed from the evangelical obsession with the year 2000), the villains of the NWA established the N.W.O. (new world order), an "apocalyptic" power shift in the script of professional wrestling. For evangelicals, the "new world order" refers to the period of time after the Rapture. More specific than "apocalypse", it refers to the harsh political and economic system established worldwide during the Great Tribulation. To use it in a meaningful sentence or two, "the Beast will establish a new world order during the Tribulation. You will be forced to take the mark of the Beast in the new world order."

The word ***gospel*** will be used a few times in this book. Its literal definition is the teaching or revelation of Jesus Christ. Many evangelical Christians seek to spread the gospel of Jesus, to preach and convert others to their faith. For them, the gospel of Jesus is the one path to eternal life in heaven. There are four books in the Bible's New Testament that detail the life of Jesus on earth. These four (Matthew, Mark, Luke and John) are known as the four gospels.

Lastly, I want to define ***Lamb*** (capital L) as in "the Lamb of God." In Jewish tradition, sacrifices were made to God for the atonement of sins. A lamb (baby sheep) was seen as a pure and innocent creature. The sacrifice and killing of a lamb and spilling of its blood was the ritual through which man received forgiveness from God. In the New Testament, Christians believe God came to earth in human form and sacrificed himself for all of mankind. Jesus Christ is known as "the Lamb of God", the pure and innocent, sinless God in the flesh. I believe Jesus died for all humanity, and through that sacrifice, man receives forgiveness for sin and is made clean in the sight of God.

Section 1 -

The Countdown to the End

The 1990s were a great time to be alive. There was so much that was new and exciting in our world, whether it be geopolitically, technologically, or in the entertainment and leisure category. The bitter Cold War had just ended with the collapse of the USSR. Freedom (and American capitalism) was spreading worldwide. Global trade increased. Early computers and video gaming systems gave us a new form of entertainment. There were blockbuster movies, sensational scandals, and even boy band groups. It was a new era! Perhaps most remarkably, the '90s began the internet revolution. AOL and Microsoft brought the internet into our daily lives and into countless households globally. Yes, thirty-five years ago, we did not have the internet. We didn't have cell phones. We didn't have around-the-clock live tv stations. Our world has changed so much.

Another unique quality of the 1990s is that it was the last decade of the millennium. As exciting as the '90s were, this quirk of the calendar also inspired fear and mystery and intrigue. Any event that happens only once every 1,000 years is sure to be momentous. But the year 2000 AD had an elephant-in-the-room cloud hanging over it. Many believed it would be the end of the world! It wasn't just preachers speaking out on this topic on Sunday mornings. The year 2000 had an ominous quality to it in secular culture at large. Many a book or disaster movie entertained the idea of calamity at the end of the millennium. Even pop music reinforced the idea, with Prince famously encouraging us all to "party like it's 1999."

To be clear, millions of people believed the world would end in the year 2000. It obviously did not happen. Yet many believe we are nevertheless still near the "end of days" and the prophesied return of Jesus to the earth. Over the next few chapters, you will learn why so many millions of evangelical Christians still believe that the end is near. You will read why the year 2000 was circled as the end for so long. You will see why many believe the exact year of 2000 was wrong but just by a bit. Specifically, the next chapters will explore the Millennial Day Theory, the prophecies of Jesus in Matthew 24, the rebirth of the nation of Israel, and an often overlooked prophecy from the book of Daniel. Lastly, an additional prophecy involving Jerusalem and the Holy Temple is also explored.

This first section is very important for context. To consider if the Antichrist is alive on earth today, it is first essential to determine if the biblical prophecies about the apocalypse are coming true. If the end of the world is not near, then the Beast is not among us yet. So the first question this book poses is simple: Is the end of the world and return of Jesus near? Is it possible? Is it?

Chapter 1: The Millenial Day Theory

Why was there such rampant speculation in evangelical Christian churches about the year 2000 being the end of the world, or the date of the Rapture, or the year that Jesus would return to earth? It seems counterintuitive that faithful Christians should even speculate about such things in the first place. In the book of Matthew, Jesus, speaks to his disciples and is very clear about his promised return to earth. In verse 36 of the 24th chapter, we read: "But of that day and hour knoweth no man, no, not the angels of heaven, but my Father only." The clear takeaway is that only God the Father knows when the end will come, the time when Jesus will return to the earth. For any man to speculate with specific dates or times seems foolhardy. To put it bluntly, any Christian who postulated that Jesus would return at the stroke of midnight on January 1, 2000 was not to be trusted. No man knows the day or the hour.

Specifics notwithstanding, the Bible does give us clues about the end of the world. Prophecies about the return of Jesus are found in both the Old and New Testaments, specifically in the book of Daniel, the four Gospels of Matthew, Mark, Luke and John, and other books such as those written to the Corinthians and Thessalonians. And of course the final book of the Bible, Revelation, is written almost entirely as a book of visions and prophecy. While it may be sacrilegious for any person to name an exact date or time of Jesus' return, it seems perfectly reasonable and appropriate for one to interpret the Bible and consider the "season" of Christ's return.

Growing up in the Church, I heard a lot of speculation about just that. I heard it from preachers and Sunday School teachers and church camp counselors and my parents. I heard all the time that the end was near, that Jesus was returning soon. More times than not, I heard that it would all likely go down by the year 2000. There were many "signs" out there that fit biblical prophecy. I will cover several of these in the following chapters. But first, why was the exact year 2000 on the radar? Perhaps many evangelical Christians themselves have never heard this biblical speculation. But I heard it often growing up, and it fascinated me. Surprisingly, the story about the "end" is rooted in the "beginning". Allow me a few more paragraphs to fill in the prerequisite backstory and connect the dots. Behold, I present the Millennial Day Theory.

The first Book of the Bible is Genesis, and in the first verses of the first chapter of Genesis, we hear the story of the creation of the earth. This story is well known even in secular culture. We read that in the beginning, God created the heavens and the earth. We go on to read that all things were created in 6 days' time. Notably, these included trees and grass created on the third day, the sun and moon created on the fourth, all birds and sea life created on the fifth, and animals and mankind created on the sixth. On the seventh day, God rested.

In modern times, we know one of three things. Either science is fiction, the creation story of Genesis is fiction, or the creation story is symbolic or otherwise not literal. Scientists have used radiometric dating to determine the earth is a few billions years old. Fossils of the dinosaurs have been dated to over 200 million years ago. Likewise, the fossils of early mammals have been dated back to hundreds of millions of years ago. Meanwhile, the earliest advanced human civilizations are only a few thousand years old. It seems that all animals and mankind were not literally created on the same day. Is science wrong? Is radiometric dating just nonsense?

We live in a world of remarkably advanced scientific understanding and application. We live in a world where high-tech satellites orbit the earth and allow us to communicate in real time with people thousands of miles away. We live in a world where we can send rockets into space, a world where we can accurately predict phenomena like eclipses and aurora and hurricane formation. Science is present and precise in countless ways in our everyday lives. The cell phones in our pockets are the result of unfathomable scientific ingenuity. Scientific truths like gravity and the earth's exact orbit endure whether one believes in them or not. Because I also choose to believe in the Bible and that God created the earth and man, I am left to conclude that yes, the creation story in Genesis is most likely symbolic and not literal. The time table just doesn't match up. And for me, that is ok. The Bible is full of symbolism. As it turns out, time itself may be fluid in the Bible too.

In 2 Peter 3:8, we read that to God, a day is like a thousand years. This same language was used in the Old Testament in Psalm 90:4, where we read "For a thousand years in your sight are like a day that has just gone by." For believers, the takeaway is that God is not bound by time. God is the Alpha and the Omega, the beginning and the end, the first and the last (Isaiah 44:6, Revelation 1:8). Again, God is not bound by our concept of time. Spending six days or billions of years to create and form the earth could be the same to God. With this understanding, it seems the creation story of Genesis need not be a literal telling of how God created all living things. So then why is the Creation story written this way? Why is it seven days long? Faithful believers know that God is the Alpha and Omega, the beginning and the end. Again, is it possible that the story of our beginning is really the timetable for the end?

As I mentioned earlier, the earliest known human civilizations and records date back a few thousand years. Specifically, scientists believe both the Sumerians of Mesopotamia (modern day Iraq) and ancient Egyptians date back to approximately 4000 BC. This seems curious that modern science would date artifacts and writings from the earliest known advanced human civilizations to almost exactly four millenia prior to the birth of Jesus Christ.

Enter the Millennial Day Theory, a notion that perhaps, just perhaps, the creation story is actually a parable for the timeline of mankind on earth. Recall that God created the earth and all living things in "six days" and rested on the seventh. Recall also from 2 Peter that to God, a day is like a thousand years. What if the story of modern man on earth is for "six days" (six thousand years), with the seventh day of rest (a final 1,000 years) separate from the first six. The theory posits that the story of man on earth is 7,000 years long, just as a week has seven days. The first 6,000 years span from early recorded human history through to the return of Christ. The last 1,000 years is the millennial reign of Christ on earth as detailed in Revelation 20:1-6.

The Millennial Day Theory gained widespread attention in some evangelical churches in the late 20th century. Carbon dating was developed in the mid 1900's. As mentioned earlier, artifacts and writings from the earliest known civilizations in the Middle East were dated to around 4000 BC. Using the Millennial Day Theory, Jesus would return to the earth 6,000 years after man was created. This put the year 2000 AD as the target date of Christ's return. Taking the theory a step further, one would surmise that Jesus first came to the earth 4,000 years after man. This would coincide with the start of the "fifth day" of the creation story. On days 5 and 6, God created life in the form of birds, sea creatures, animals and humans. Similarly, Jesus came to earth to bring life - eternal life - to all who believe. Again, on the 7th day, God rested. Per the Millennial Day Theory, this coincides with the return of Christ to the earth to rule for a final 1,000 years. After that, the symbolic week ends, and so does human history. A new heaven and earth are created for all those who believe in the Lord Jesus Christ, and the faithful live with God for eternity.

Many evangelicals today still consider the Millennial Day Theory a possibility. Modern historians place the earliest human civilizations *around* the year 4000 BC, but it is not an exact date. For example, if the story of modern man on earth really began in 3975 BC, that would move the end of the 6th millennium to 2025 AD.

Others believe Jesus will return exactly 2,000 years after his death and resurrection, as opposed to 2,000 years after his birth. It would be fittingly symbolic of that death and resurrection. In the Bible, Jesus died, stayed dead for two days, and arose back to life at the dawn of the third day. Using the Millennial Day Theory, one could extrapolate Jesus leaving the earth for exactly 2,000 years (just like he was dead for two days). The exact date of Jesus' death is not known with historical certainty. Based on the reign of Pontius Pilate and that the crucifixion occurred during Passover, the best estimates place the death of Jesus on Friday, April 3, 33 AD. If this date is accurate, proponents of the Millennial Day theory could hypothesize a return of Jesus in the year 2033 AD. Some theorists have the year 2026 circled for the

Rapture, assuming a seven year Tribulation. Like a broken record, I again stress that no man knows the day or hour of the return of the Lord.

To be clear, the Bible in no way explicitly teaches or spells out the Millennial Day Theory. It may be based on many verses and themes in the Bible, but it certainly involves a great deal of biblical conjecture and symbolism. In my youth, I recall it being discussed by a pastor as a possibility, never an absolute. Nevertheless, for many evangelicals, it explains why there was a bullseye on the year 2000.

Ultimately, the Millennial Day theory is just one piece of the "end times" puzzle. The Bible contains many other prophecies about when to expect the return of Jesus. For many evangelicals, these other "signs of the times" also seemed to be relevant around the year 2,000, and they seem to be even more relevant today.

Chapter 2: Signs of the Times

A good amount of Biblical prophecy is cryptic, relying heavily on symbolism and obscure details. Some of the most direct prophecies about the end times, however, come from the lips of Jesus Christ himself. During his time on earth with his disciples, Jesus makes it clear he will be betrayed, put to death, be resurrected from the dead, and then leave the earth. It is foretold that he will come to the earth again at the end of ages. In Matthew 24, Jesus' disciples ask him point blank "what will be the sign of your coming (again) and of the end of the age?" In verse 5, we learn that there will be deceivers who come in the name of Jesus but then claim "I am the Messiah" and fool many. In verse 6, we read "You will hear of wars and rumors of wars, but see to it that you are not alarmed. Such things must happen, but the end is still to come." Verses 7 and 8 continue "Nation will rise against nation, and kingdom against kingdom. There will be famines and earthquakes in various places. All these are the beginning of birth pains." Verse 14 indicates that for the end to come, the gospel of Jesus must "be proclaimed throughout the whole world as a testimony to all nations."

As mentioned above, Jesus references deceivers who come in his name as a sign of the end. Of course, this book is fundamentally about a great deceiver, about the one who comes in the name of Jesus but eventually claims "I am the Messiah." In both Christian and secular culture at large, this figure is the Antichrist. The Bible also identifies this figure as "the Man of Lawlessness." In the Book of Revelation, he is "the Beast." He will have his own unique mark or trademark associated with the number 666. The ensuing chapters will cover the Beast in great detail, but suffice to say the emergence of the deceptive Beast on the scene is a sure sign of Jesus' return. The emergence of a powerful, influential man who takes on a Messianic persona could be a fulfillment of Matthew 24:5.

The reference to "wars and rumors of wars" is one of the most well-known prophecies about the end of days. For starters, it just makes a lot of practical sense, especially given the proliferation of nuclear weapons. Indeed, this contributed greatly to speculation that the world could end around the year 2000. The biggest wars the world has ever seen occurred in the 20th century, including World War I and World War II. Of course, World War II ended with the use of nuclear weapons by the United States against Japan. The Cold War and nuclear standoff between the USA and USSR ensued shortly thereafter and lasted for decades. Generations grew up afraid of nuclear war. Just as today's schoolkids and youth have "active shooter drills" in the classroom, the generations before us grew up with "duck and cover drills." Untold millions of people grew up afraid of a nuclear Armageddon.

Since World War II, humanity has seen a continuation of consequential 'wars and rumors of war' around the globe. The Cold War and its nuclear fears lasted from the 1950s through to the end of the 1980s. There was the Korean War in the 1950s, the Vietnam War in the 60s and 70s, and seemingly one conflict or another in the Middle East/ Holy Land in most any decade for the last century. This includes the seemingly never ending conflict between the Israelis and Palestenians. At the time of publishing, the current conflict between Hamas and Israel has many predicting doomsday yet again. Overall, many argue that the words of Jesus have been fulfilled over the past 80 years. Nation has risen up against nation. We hear of wars and rumors of war constantly.

As noted above, another sign of the 'end of the world' is that there will be famines and earthquakes. There have of course been a multitude of these over the past 75 years or so. Earthquakes are nothing new to the earth. One could easily dismiss this 'prophecy' as being applicable to any time period ever. What is different over the last few decades, though, is the sheer magnitude of devastation they have caused. The human population of the earth has quadrupled over the past century, from under 2 billion in 1920 to over 8 billion in 2024. Famines in Africa, the Middle East, and Asia have killed tens of millions.The world's deadliest known earthquakes have occurred over the past few decades, including in Haiti in 2010 and Sumatra in 2004. Millions were killed, injured, or displaced. Modern natural disasters in heavily populated areas seem more consequential, perhaps, than isolated events centuries ago affecting less-populated rural regions.

For many who insist we may be nearing the end of days, it does seem like there are more weather events and natural disasters and famines and droughts worldwide. Hurricanes and tornadoes seem much more common and more ferocious. Wildfires are scorching the earth at a record pace, even in the Amazon rainforest. Scientists are warning of irreversible climate change that could threaten human survival in future centuries. Also, it does feel like there are wars and rocket strikes and threats of international combat all the time. The Mideast and Holy Land are as fraught with conflict and instability as ever.

The key part of the passage in Matthew, however, seems to often be overlooked. The first three words of Matthew 24:6 state "You will hear." Let that sink in. It isn't just that earthquakes and famines and weather calamities and wars are happening more regularly. A key point is that in today's world, we *hear* about these events on the regular. We didn't hear of worldwide events centuries ago, but we do now. We hear about them and see video footage and hear witness testimonials and hear from reporters on the scene. We have the technology and infrastructure in place to hear about potential prophetic events coming to pass. Earthquakes that nobody heard about or knew about are maybe not prophetic. Seeing humans around the globe constantly battling war and natural disasters hits differently. To spell it out clearly, Jesus' disciples would not have "heard" about an earthquake or war on a different continent. We hear about it today in real time.

Again, in Matthew 24:14, Jesus indicates that for the end to come, the gospel must be proclaimed to all people worldwide. Is this prophecy closer than ever to being fulfilled? Sure, there have been missionaries worldwide for decades, preaching and sharing about their faith in Jesus. But here in the 21st century, for the first time, anyone in most any country could now stumble upon the gospel of Jesus simply with a computer or smartphone. The internet and wifi connectivity have made this a reality. There are even artificial intelligence apps that theoretically could translate the words of Jesus and the Bible into any language. Within a few years, satellite wifi will enable internet connectivity to every inch of the globe.

Ultimately, it is for the reader to decide if the prophetic words of Jesus in Matthew 24 have been fulfilled or are being fulfilled. One thing is clear - many evangelical Christians absolutely believed it leading up to the year 2000. Indeed, at the time of publishing, many still do.

Chapter 3: The Chosen Generation

Many of the biblical prophecies or pieces of prophecies previously mentioned have become ingrained in mainstream culture. Of course, the mark of the Beast and the number 666 are household terms. Things like wars and geopolitical instability, especially in the Middle East/ Holy Land, inspire talks of the apocalypse among believers and non-believers alike. You likely have heard this recently, what with the brutal conflict (at time of publishing) between Hamas and Hezbollah and Israel. Other issues not directly mentioned in the Bible also alarm millions about an impending apocalypse, including the proliferation of nuclear weapons, the climate crisis, the emergence of artificial intelligence, etc etc. But two prophecies contained in the Bible have garnered much less attention in secular culture at large. Neither is found in the book of Revelation, but both of these prophetic nuggets in Scripture could suggest we are indeed living at the end of days. These prophecies have been preached from evangelical pulpits for decades. Millions believe them. If true, both these prophecies could confirm that the Man of Lawlessness, the great Beast of Revelation, is among us now.

Growing up, I recall my parents telling me that their generation, the baby-boomers, would live to see the return of Jesus. It was in the Bible! Specifically, I was told this: the Bible said that the generation born or alive at the time of Israel's rebirth/statehood would live to see the return of Jesus. Israel as a home for the Jews had been under foreign control for millenia, including by the Romans at the time of Jesus' life on earth. In AD 70, the Jews became scattered, driven out from their homeland. And so Israel remained until the 20th century. Per a decree from the UN, Israel became an official state/nation on May 14, 1948.

This was the literal fulfillment of prophecy, or so I was told. As I grew older and heard this prophecy repeatedly, I decided to read this for myself. We didn't have internet search engines back then, so my quest for knowledge took a while. I couldn't find these Bible verses anywhere! Did the Bible really say this?

In Matthew chapter 24 (as well as Mark 13 and Luke 21), Jesus discusses with his disciples his second coming to Earth. This is the return of Jesus at the end of days, at the end of the great Tribulation. Jesus offered up several signs that would signal his return was near. As discussed in the last chapter, these signs include wars and rumors of wars, earthquakes, and famines. Other signs include the gospel being preached worldwide (verse 14), and various signs in the sky or heavens, such as the stars falling, the moon losing its light, and the sun being blocked out (verse 29). In the same chapter after listing these signs of the times, Jesus teaches the parable of the fig tree. In Matthew 24:32-34, we read "Now learn this parable from the fig tree: When its branch has already become tender and put forth its leaves, you know that summer is near. So you also, when you see these things, know that it is near - at the doors! Assuredly, I say to you, this generation will by no means pass away till all these things take place." But what does this parable have to do with Israel and its statehood?

While it is possible Jesus just happened to use the fig tree in his prophetic parable randomly (a horticultural analogy lacking any deeper meaning), many see this as a clear reference to Israel and the Jewish people. My parents certainly did! It turns out that the fig tree or the fruit on a fig tree is used repeatedly in the Bible as a symbolic reference to Israel and the Jewish people. In Hosea 9:10, the "fathers of Israel" are referred to as "the first fruits on the fig tree." Later in Jeremiah 24, the Jewish people of Judah are being driven out to Babylon. They are referred to as good figs and bad figs, depending on their relationship to God. In Matthew 21 and Luke 13, Jesus encounters and curses a barren fig tree, as it bears no fruit. Shortly after in chapter 23 of Matthew, he addresses the hypocrisy and failures of the Pharisees and rabbis leading the Jewish people astray. In Jeremiah 8, God warns the people of Jerusalem (through the prophet Jeremiah) that unless they repent, Jerusalem would be destroyed and they would be driven out. In verse 13, we read that "There will be no figs on the tree, and their leaves will wither." The use of the fig tree allegory appears in Micah 4:4 in a description of the "last days" (Micah 4:1), but the clear connection to Israel is missing in this occurrence. Nevertheless, many scholars and believers accept the parable of the fig tree in Matthew 24 as more accurately the parable of Israel as the fig tree.

Viewing the parable with this deeper meaning, the rebirth of Israel as a nation is interpreted as the fig tree budding again, putting forth its leaves. For believers, this is a sign that the return of Jesus is near. Again, Israel was reborn into statehood in AD 1948. The Jewish people were driven out of their homeland in AD 70, a few decades after the crucifixion of Jesus. For nearly 2 millenia, the Jewish people were scattered around the globe with no official homeland. That is no longer the case. Modern Israel is 76 years old at the time of publishing. It follows that the people born at the time of Israel's rebirth are also in their 70s. If any of them are to live to see the return of Jesus, time is running out.

To recap and spell it out clearly, the Bible does not directly say that the statehood of Israel in 1948 was a 100% infallible sign that Jesus is returning soon. It doesn't say that the generation born then would live to see Jesus' return. My parents took the possibly symbolic words of the Bible and of preachers and simplified things into an absolute. The Bible is not so clear or direct. Nevertheless, for many believers, the parable of the fig tree and the symbolic use of figs and fig trees to represent both the Jewish people and Jewish state (Israel) is compelling. Taken together with all the other "signs of the times" spelled out by the prophets and Jesus himself, the case is perhaps more compelling.

There is a second nugget of prophecy that has also not permeated throughout mainstream secular culture. But growing up in the church, I heard about it all the time. The book of Daniel in the Old Testament is a book containing many prophecies. Many sections of the book correspond with and match up to John's prophetic visions in Revelation. In Daniel 12:4, we read "But thou, O Daniel, shut up the words and seal the book, even to the time of the end: many shall run to and fro, and knowledge shall be increased." Many believers have interpreted these words in our modern world. They assert that just before the end of days, humanity as a collective will experience and enjoy a vast increase in knowledge and travel. They assert that we are living in those days now. Are we?

To spell it out clearly, the interpretation of many evangelicals is this - Daniel mentions the end and describes it as a time that people will move about "to and fro" (travel?) and that knowledge (technology and innovation?) will be increased. This interpretation fits the narrative that we are in the end times now. Of course a modest increase in knowledge, innovation, and travel began in the Middle Ages and gained momentum with the Industrial Revolution of the 18th and 19th centuries. But specifically, the life of mankind on earth really began to seriously advance after World War II, after the Holocaust, right about the time Israel was becoming a state.

Think about it. How much has the life of the average human changed over the last 75 years? Let's start with travel. The changes for humanity in travel during this time are profound. Back in the day, most people rarely left the area where they lived and worked. But now? We travel frequently and all over the place. The invention and modernization of cars, cruise ships, and airplanes have changed everything. Many of us have flown or sailed far away from our homes for leisure fun. Many people fly regularly for work. The world has changed so much. One could imagine if a man like the prophet Daniel from millenia ago were to stand in a busy airport terminal, he could very well describe the scene as "many will run to and fro." We have flown humans into outer space to live on the space station. Humans have walked on the moon, and plans are in the works to send humans to Mars and beyond. We live in a different time.

Likewise, the increase in "knowledge" over the past 75 years is undeniable and obvious. Of course, this increase in technology led to the aforementioned transportation marvels. But the increase in human enlightenment and ingenuity also applies to most every field of study: physics, chemistry, engineering, medicine, architecture, etc etc. Technology has revolutionized modern life in every way, from how we communicate, how we work, even how we meet friends and potential mates. A time traveler from 1945 would be floored to see all the modern gadgets we have today. As just one example, imagine their surprise to see all the power and knowledge and capabilities almost all of us carry in our pockets daily. We can do most anything simply with a cell phone and invisible internet connection. It is like technological magic - we are wizards Harry! We can order (and have delivered) food and goods and gifts. We can manage our finances. We can facetime chat in real time with people in most any time zone anywhere. The list goes on and on.

Moreover, we get to enjoy these modern marvels longer because we are living longer. Advances in modern medicine have extended our expected life spans compared to the generations in previous centuries. We have medicines and antibiotics to treat infections. We have screening tools to detect (and thus treat) diseases. We have advanced techniques in surgery to treat and cure ailments that were previously untreatable. We have greater knowledge and understanding of the things that can maximize our lifespans, and how to incorporate these things into our lives (think nutrition, exercise, avoiding carcinogens, etc). We are living in an amazing, unprecedented era of rapid technological advancement, a time of understanding and awareness, an age of a clear "increase in knowledge" if you will.

There is another side to that "increase in knowledge." With our advances in technology in the 20th century came new threats. As anyone who sat through the Barbenheimer double feature knows, nuclear weapons were first developed and used in the 1940s. As mentioned previously, this development led to understandable apocalyptic fears in secular culture at large. For the first time, humans had the power to destroy the earth through nuclear weapons of mass destruction. In theory, if a wide scale nuclear war broke out on earth, a nuclear winter could ensue and eradicate human life on earth.

In the 21st century, our technology is continuing to advance at a rapid pace. Artificial intelligence is beginning to reshape our lives even as I write. For now, it is being implemented in seemingly harmless, innocuous ways - assisting with internet searches, completing simple tasks through voice recognition, etc. But fears persist that science fiction is becoming reality too fast. It is not hard to envision large nations (and bad actors) further increasing their military might through "intelligent" robotic troops and drones. Yes, we live in a changing world, and fears of apocalyptic doom are not reserved for just the church faithful.

Is this what the prophet Daniel envisioned? Was he shown a glimpse of our fast-paced, modern world of extraordinary technology and travel? Did he see a world where advanced militaries and weapons could literally destroy the earth? Some say no, it is just modern day prognosticators looking to justify their narrative. Daniel could be referring to spiritual knowledge and maturity. "Running to and fro" does not necessarily mean travel or military movement. As with much of biblical prophecy, it is hard to know. The verses are vague and can be interpreted many ways.

However, some see Daniel's words differently. For them, his specific mention of the end times is important, and the mention of increases in knowledge and people moving to and fro may not just be random. As mentioned elsewhere in this book, it isn't just that Daniel mentions these concepts as an aside. Rather, when taken in the complete fullness of the end times picture, these two prophecies have a distinct purpose. It is the ability of people (and militaries) to travel worldwide quickly that could enable the prophesied global military state that the Beast will preside over. It is this increase and ease of travel that could allow the Beast himself to rule from anywhere, allowing visits to the Holy Land and Jerusalem. It is the extreme increase in knowledge and technology that could facilitate the reign of the Beast worldwide.

He would be able to use modern communication devices to rule in real time. It is the increase in technological know-how that could enable a one-world digital currency.

Likewise, the prophecy that all people everywhere will hear the gospel of Jesus Christ (Matthew 24:14) is only now possible through these very increases in technological knowledge and ease of travel. When taken in this context, the prophetic words of Daniel have a very practical purpose - the increase in knowledge and travel in the end times is a conduit to the fulfillment of the rest of prophecy. Moreover, the increase in knowledge has led to the aforementioned expansion of the average lifespan. If one were to believe that a large population of people born around the time of Israel's rebirth in 1948 will live to see Jesus' return, they will have to live a long life, longer than most people did in the previous centuries. It is only through the vast increases in medical knowledge that this is even possible.

Throughout this book, I am making a direct attempt not just to mention various prophecies and "signs of the times", but to appreciate and explore the very practical reasons they may exist. In this context, the prophecies of Daniel could seem most relevant and applicable to this very moment in time. It isn't just that travel and knowledge could be increased just before the return of Jesus; rather, these prophetic tidbits have a specific purpose as mentioned above. It could very well be that these are two more pieces of the puzzle that seem perfectly in place for the Beast of Revelation to begin his reign.

Chapter 4 - The Holy Land

You have already read it in this book. You may have heard it from coworkers or neighbors or relatives. You've likely seen it on social media. Every time there is conflict in the Middle East and Israel specifically, people say it is a sign of the times. Some say Jesus is returning soon. Why do people think like this? What Biblical prophecies refer to Jerusalem?

Exploring and analyzing all of the Bible's prophecies related to Jerusalem and Jesus could be its own extensive book. The Old Testament is chock full of all kinds of prophecies. For Christian believers, many of these have already been fulfilled. Christians believe the prophesied Messiah has already come to earth once, that Messiah being Jesus Christ.

This book is obviously laser-focused on "end times" prophecies and the coming Beast of Revelation. In analyzing Scripture, it can be difficult to decipher if a prophecy has already been fulfilled, or if it is a reference to future events just before the end of the world. As such, this chapter will only scratch the surface of how Jerusalem figures into the end times' equation as relates to the Beast.

The Holy Temple, or Temple of Jerusalem, was historically the center of worship and culture in ancient Israel. The First Temple was completed in 957 BCE under the reign of King Solomon, the Son of King David. It was built on Mount Moriah, or the Temple Mount, a site of great significance for the Israelites going back to the days of Abraham, Isaac and Jacob. The Ark of the Covenant and every other important Jewish relic and Scriptures were housed here. The First Temple became the most important site in all of ancient Israel, the focal point of worship and sacrifices. The First Temple was torn down and destroyed in 587 BC during the reign of Nebuchadnezzar II.

The Second Temple was built on the same site and completed in 515 BC under the rule of Cyrus II. Glossing over a lot of history, a damaged Second Temple was rebuilt during the time of Jesus' birth and life under the rule of King Herod. It was eventually fully destroyed, this time in 70 AD during the First Roman-Jewish War. The war began in 66 AD under the reign of Roman Emperor Nero. At the time, it was speculated by some that Nero was the prophesied Antichrist.

Today in the 21st century, the Temple Mount (and Jerusalem itself) is the most contested piece of real estate on earth. It has religious and cultural significance for Jews, Muslims, and Christians alike. The Jewish people were driven out of Israel in 70 AD. Midway through that millennium, the Islamic Dome of the Rock and al-Aqsa mosque were built on the Temple Mount. It still stands today in that spot. All that remains of the Second Jewish Temple is the Western Wall, also known as the Wailing Wall, which sits adjacent to the Al-Aqsa mosque complex.

So how does this all tie into the Biblical "end of the world" picture? Key Scriptures seem to indicate (or can be interpreted to indicate) that the Antichrist will eventually exalt himself as God in the Holy Temple in Jerusalem. In Daniel 9, we read about what has been coined "the seventy weeks of Daniel." It is a prophecy with elements that came true, in that the Holy Temple was indeed rebuilt in Jerusalem (in 515 BC). Many evangelicals interpret that 69 of the prophesied 70 weeks have come to pass. The final "week" (interpreted as seven years) is the seven-year Tribulation, a time when the Temple could be rebuilt on the Holy Mount for a third time. When the Beast finally exalts himself as God in the

Temple, this is the prophesied "abomination of desolation" in Daniel 9:27.

Jesus references this "abomination of desolation" in Matthew 24:15. This is in response to his disciples asking about when he will return and the end of times. The Beast posing as Christ in the Temple is a final sign of the return of Jesus. This is reinforced in II Thessalonians 2. In verses 3 and 4, Paul writes about the return of Jesus and the end times. "Do not let anyone deceive you in any way, for that day will not come until the rebellion occurs and the man of lawlessness is revealed, the man doomed to destruction. He will oppose and exalt himself over everything that is called God or is worshiped, so that he sets himself up in God's temple, proclaiming himself to be God."

At the time of publishing, this prophecy is problematic. If interpreted literally, this prophecy is nowhere near fulfillment. It seems a third Holy Temple would have to be built on the Temple Mount. In today's geopolitical world, this would not appear to be happening anytime soon. Any endeavor to relocate or destroy or demolish the al-Aqsa mosque would set off immediate war in the Middle East, a war which would likely expand worldwide. If the prophesied Beast did indeed seek to drive out Muslim interests from this holy site, one thing is clear - the Beast would have to be pro-Israeli and anti-Palestenian. The prophesied Beast would have to want to wipe out the Palestenians. Then and only then could the Holy Temple be rebuilt. If this came to pass, the Beast would support it at first before desecrating it with his demands for self-worship.

If this prophecy is interpreted a bit more loosely, one could imagine a Third Holy Temple being commissioned nearby the original site or at a different site of Biblical significance. Another interpretation is that the Beast will desecrate the site through self-aggrandizement regardless of whether the Temple is rebuilt. One way or another, Scripture is clear that the blasphemous Beast will commit a sacrilege and eventually demand to be worshiped as mankind's savior.

Again, this is but a very shallow overview of the role of Israel and the Holy Land in Biblical prophecy. Still, it should provide context as to why instability and war in the Middle East causes apprehension for those anticipating the Biblical apocalypse. Any war or rocket strikes in Jerusalem could ultimately be the catalyst for the end of days, for how the Beast sets his sights and attention on the Holy Land.

Section 2 -

The Apocalypse

As outlined at the beginning of this book, the "end of the world" in the Bible is not a singular event. Rather, many believe a series of events will transpire that culminate with Jesus returning to earth. This section will touch on each of these: the Rapture, Tribulation, and Great Tribulation. According to Scripture, it is during this time that the Beast of Revelation will come into full worldwide power. He will have a right-hand man, an enabler described as the second beast or "false prophet." This section will introduce the false prophet as described in the Bible. Lastly, this section will conclude with important info about the Antichrist, dispelling the myth that he is Satan in the flesh.

Just like the previous chapters, this second section is pivotal for establishing context - the setting in which the Beast will reign. These chapters are fairly short but vitally important. They set up the explosive observations in section 3 about both the prophesied Beast and the red-hatted politician.

Chapter 5: The Rapture

The Rapture - It is a word I have heard all of my life. My preacher, my youth pastor, my parents, and my Sunday School teachers all talked about the Rapture. I needed to stay on the straight and narrow path of righteousness, for the hour was near. The Rapture could happen at any moment. But what is it, and is it even biblical? Evangelical Protestants sure believe it is real and that it is an integral piece in the end times puzzle, in the latter days just before Jesus returns. If you are unfamiliar with this term or its implications, this chapter will provide some insight and opinion. If you already know about the Rapture in the evangelical tradition, read on for a refresher. This chapter is an integral piece in laying the groundwork for the rest of this book and its shocking analysis of our world at this very moment in time.

At the end of the movie Avengers: Infinity War, the powerful villain Thanos changes the history of the world in an instant. He has obtained all the so-called "infinity stones" and completed a powerful weapon (a large, bedazzled glove). With all the stones in place, Thanos dramatically snaps his giant fingers. From there, chaos quickly unfolds. It turns out that this "snap heard 'round the world" has the power to eradicate one half of the earth's population. Within seconds, half of all humans randomly cease to exist, evaporating into a pile of dust. We see the immediate implications of this cataclysmic event in the final scene with character Nick Fury. Cars everywhere begin to crash, suddenly driverless. Planes and helicopters fall from the sky, suddenly pilot-less. There are fiery explosions all around. Family and friends go missing and cannot be found. Nobody knows what is happening. The immediate danger, chaos, confusion and shock for those left alive on earth gives way to long-term grief, suffering and lingering bewilderment. The world has changed forever. This plot may seem dramatic and original, but if you grew up in an evangelical Christian household, this sounds a lot like the Rapture.

In terms of the apocalypse and end times, the Rapture is a distinct event, a sudden moment in time. At the Rapture, all faithful followers of Christ (as judged and determined by God the Father) will be taken from the earth in the blink of an eye. They will be caught up or snatched from the earth while still alive and join those who have already died but are resurrected in Christ. The concept of the Rapture comes from 1 Thessalonians 4:17, which reads "Then we which are alive and remain shall be caught up together with them in the clouds, to meet the Lord in the air; and so shall we ever be with the Lord." Being caught up in the air seems to be a distinct event from Jesus' second coming onto earth. In John 14:3, it reads "And if I go and prepare a place for you, I will come back and take you to be with me that you also may be where I am." Importantly in Revelation 3:10, John hears in his vision "Since you have kept my command to endure patiently, I will also keep you from the hour of trial that is going to come on the whole world to test the inhabitants of the earth." This verse, when interpreted as being directed to the devout believers at the end of days, seems to indicate a rapture or reaping of believers just before the Tribulation.

It turns out the literal English word "Rapture" in this sense is not biblical - it simply does not appear anywhere in the Bible as it relates to prophecy. And yet, many evangelical Christians, particularly in America, believe in the Rapture as much as they believe in Jesus, Mary and Joseph. Based on Scripture, "the Reaping" or "the Snatching" would be a more accurate term, but these sound a bit too much like a horror film. The term "rapture" comes from the Greek 'harpazo' found in the aforementioned verses (before translation), meaning to "seize" or "snatch away." For believers, the Bible implies it will happen separate from Jesus' second coming, that there will be a reaping of living souls from the earth.

The modern notion took root in the 1830's by a British teacher and cleric named John Nelson Darby, but it was really popularized in the mid to late 20th century in American evangelical circles. Early works like the movie "A Thief in the Night" or the book "the Late Great Planet Earth" portrayed the Rapture in contemporary times, complete with people vanishing and worldwide chaos a la Thanos' snap. Influential preachers, tele-evangelists, and commentators like Billy Graham, Jerry Fallwell, Pat Robertson, Jim Bakker, John Hagge and Jack van Impe preached and taught about the Rapture to millions.

In the late 1990's and into the new millennium, the book series (and later film series) "Left Behind" capitalized on Y2K apocalyptic fears and introduced a new generation to the Rapture. As alluded to earlier, the Rapture could theoretically happen at any moment. True believers in Christ who are alive could vanish, resulting in driverless cars and confused non-believers literally left behind. This is how it is portrayed in "Left Behind", and the book series has sold over 80 million copies. These books and movies brought the concept of the Rapture out of the church and into the consciousness of mainstream culture.

Among different branches of Christianity, there is great uncertainty and discrepancies about the timing of the Rapture. I grew up being taught it would happen before the Tribulation, a seven-year period of increasing trials and tribulations on earth (discussed in the next chapter). This is a common belief among many evangelicals, and it is how the Rapture is portrayed in most of the aforementioned works like the "Left Behind" series. Theologians and clergy who subscribe to this view cite many biblical reasons. As so much of prophecy is not straight-forward and instead relies on symbolism or appears in Jesus' parables, there are many passages that can be interpreted to support this pre-tribulation Rapture timeline, even if the Bible does not spell it out clearly. The most easily cited rationale involves the Church not being mentioned in Revelation after Chapter 3. The entirety of the seven year Tribulation and the trials and torments involved under the Beast leave out the Church completely. It seems true believers at the start of the Tribulation will not be on earth, and as mentioned Revelation 3:10 spells this out clearly.

This book will assume a pre-Tribulation Rapture, the most common belief among born-again evangelicals. As mentioned repeatedly, biblical prophecy is often abstract and can be interpreted several ways. Some Christians believe in a mid-Tribulation Rapture or even no Rapture at all, that the faithful just join Jesus in the clouds at the time of his second coming (after the Tribulation). That debate is for a different book.

Assuming the Rapture occurs just before the Tribulation, it is generally believed to happen "like a thief in the night" (1 Thessalonians 5) - instantaneous and without immediate warning. Only true believers and followers of Christ will be spared from the seven year Tribulation and "caught up" or "snatched up" in the air to meet Christ along with those believers who have died over the centuries beforehand. Again, this is not the full Second Coming of Christ, which happens after the seven year Tribulation. Rather, this is the figurative Church (a collection of all individual believers, not a church building) being removed from the earth.

Evangelical Christians generally believe that not just anyone who ever went to church or "identifies'' as Christian on a survey will be raptured away. Indeed, it is reserved only for true believers in Christ - those who have accepted Jesus into their heart and soul as their Savior and have been "born again" through Christ. It is not enough to simply attend a church or do charitable works like volunteering to feed the homeless. To be "saved" (and spend eternity with God in heaven) and thus eligible to be raptured is simply to profess Jesus as Lord and Savior. It then follows that a saved person's life and actions will match the profession of faith, that they will be filled with the Holy Spirit and try to avoid sin and ask forgiveness/repent consistently, that their actions and speech and life is in a manner consistent with the teachings of Jesus. Presumably at the Rapture, these faithful believers will vanish from the earth and non-believers will be left behind, as will "Christians" who didn't make the cut or were not deemed true believers, to be blunt.

This is but a brief primer of the Rapture as has been taught in evangelical churches for decades. It is the long-awaited event that many evangelicals still expect to happen at any time. It is the moment that changes everything, the end of life as we know it today. It is the gateway to the Tribulation, a time of hell on earth.

Chapter 6: The Tribulation

Like many people, I remember the first haunted house I went in as a kid. It was at a small grocery store of all places, and the employees had set up a couple "rooms" made from big beach tents and black visqueen or tarps. I remember walking into the dimly lit space. There were big creepy plastic spiders, a witch, her foggy cauldron, a skeleton, etc. I also remember getting candy at the end. Kit-Kats make everything better! The whole thing was pretty low-budget but fun. It wasn't that scary. From then on, I always enjoyed a good haunted house at an amusement park or county fair or even at school carnivals. They weren't that scary either.

Years later, I visited a different type of haunt. It was an 'alternative' October attraction put on by a local church. Apparently, these were all the rage in the Bible Belt in the '80s and '90s. It was called "Tribulation House" and was elaborately staged inside a church recreation hall. We must have waited over an hour outside in line. Half the town was there. I remember the first room. Our group was told by live actors that people around the globe were reported missing. They had just vanished! The authorities were baffled. In another room, a group of people were meeting in secret. They had been unfaithful church folk in the past, but they realized what was going on and why their relatives were missing - the Rapture had happened! They had been left behind! Repenting their sinful ways, they had turned to God, but they had to be careful and discreet. In the next scene, I understood why they met in secret. I saw camo-clad troops. The world was a very different place and seemed to be run like a dictatorship or military state. A new authority had decreed that all citizens take his mark. I watched as some of the actors had this mark, a microchip, fake injected into their right hands. Others refused the mark and were persecuted and hauled off for execution. I remember all the yelling, the screaming, the drama of it all. In the next scene we saw the faithful who were persecuted get their eternal reward. They gained eternity in heaven. I remember these actors dressed like angels in this heavenly room. That was pretty much it for 'Tribulation House'. It scared the hell out of me.

Many evangelicals believe in the Tribulation. Growing up, I was taught that it would be a seven year period of time, the last seven years of mankind on earth before the second coming of Christ. The Rapture would happen first, and then the Tribulation would begin shortly thereafter. I was taught a lot of what I had seen in that scary 'Tribulation House'. During the seven years, mankind would experience trials and tribulations (hence the name) unlike any experienced on the earth before. There would be intense natural phenomena (earthquakes, floods, famines, hordes of locusts, hailstorms, etc.) Stars would be falling from the sky and mankind would run for the caves for safety.

During this time, a world leader would rise up to rule over all humanity. This man was the Beast, better known as the Antichrist. He would establish calm amid the chaos, but then begin his authoritarian rule. There would be one universal form of payment for all goods, and the Beast's mark was required. Those who refused the mark would be persecuted. Conditions on earth would continue to deteriorate. Any remaining Christians would be executed for their faith. Around the end of the seven years, Jesus would return to earth from the heavens in all his shining glory. The Beast would be defeated at the Battle of Armageddon.

This next part may sound familiar. My parents always made Biblical prophecy sound so absolute, like there was no ambiguity to it. There would be a Tribulation and it would be seven years long. Period. In my adult years, I of course delved through the Bible to read all about this Tribulation. And of course, I couldn't exactly find the verses that spelled it all out so neatly. As it turned out, the Bible was once again very murky as to the specifics about the Tribulation - how long it was, when exactly it would occur, and what exactly to expect. It's hard to know what is symbolic and what is literal.

The prophecies referencing a tribulation period for mankind are found in the books of Matthew and Revelation. The prophecies in the book of Daniel are involved as well. As discussed previously, Jesus' disciples ask him directly about the end days. Jesus describes wars and rumors of wars, earthquakes, famines, great wickedness, false prophets, false Messiahs, and nation turning against nation. At that time, great tribulation will pour over the earth, "great distress, unequaled from the beginning of the world until now, and never to be equaled again" (Matthew 24:21). Per verse 29, "the sun will be darkened, and the moon will not give its light; the stars will fall from the sky."

The Book of Revelation paints a very similar picture. It is hard to know if Revelation is written in pure chronological order, or if it is just a haphazard snapshot of all the things to come, as seen by the apostle John in his visions. Regardless, many perilous events are envisioned. In chapter 6, there are earthquakes, stars falling from the heavens, the sun and moon going dark, and great panic among all humanity. In chapter 8, there are storms of hail, fire, and blood raining down on the earth, destroying much vegetation. "Something like a great mountain burning with fire" ravages the seas, turning the water blood red and killing sea life. A great "star" falls from above, seemingly poisoning a portion of the earth's fresh water. In chapter 9, the sun and moon are darkened by great smoke, and swarms of locusts appear with stingers like scorpions, tormenting mankind for months. A great army of 200 million also appears, and "out of their mouths came fire, smoke, and brimstone." John states that "by these three plagues a third of mankind was killed."

(As an aside, here is how the bizarre visions in Revelation as listed above can actually make sense in our modern world. Referring to the previous paragraph, the sun and moon going dark could be eclipses or nuclear fallout in the atmosphere. Storms of hail, fire and blood sound like modern airstrikes/missile attacks. A "great mountain burning with fire" and affecting the seas with blood-red color could be a volcano. A great "star" falling to earth and poisoning the water could be a nuclear bomb. A great army with "mouths" spewing "fire, smoke, and brimstone" could be tanks or modern ground war weapons in general. In this context, these Tribulation visions in Revelation don't sound so crazy after all.)

In chapter 13, two beasts emerge, one from the sea and one from the earth. The first Beast is also known as the Man of Lawlessness or the Antichrist. He will gain full dominion over the earth, as "Authority was given to him over every tribe, tongue, and nation" (Revelation 13:7). Curiously, Revelation 13:3 suggests the beast may have a "mortal head wound" which has healed. The world will marvel at this first Beast. The second beast "exercises all the authority of the first beast in his presence, and causes the earth and all who dwell in it to worship the (first) beast" (Revelation 13:12). This second beast is also referred to as the "false prophet" and is depicted as a powerful 'right-hand man' of the Antichrist. In Revelation 13:16-18, we read about the mark of the Beast. Much more will be discussed later about these men and that mark.

CHAPTER 6: THE TRIBULATION

In chapters 14-18 of Revelation, further calamity on earth is described, much of it similar to the trials and torments mentioned above, only more extreme. It is unclear whether John is rehashing the same plagues as earlier but with further context regarding the beasts, or if these are similar but separate, more horrific occurrences. In the end, any who accept the mark of the Beast experience the full wrath of God. "If anyone worships the beast and his image, and receives his mark on his forehead or on his hand, he himself shall also drink of the wine of the wrath of God...He shall be tormented with fire and brimstone in the presence of the holy angels and in the presence of the Lamb" (Revelation 14:9-10). The Bible is very clear that one must never, ever under any circumstance receive the mark of the Beast.

There is much debate in the religious world about just how long this time of tribulation will last. I always heard at church that it would last for seven years. Many argue it will only last for three and a half years. There are merits for both timetables found in the Bible, and I will very briefly touch on those below. Ultimately, this book is not about how long the Tribulation is or is not, and as such I will not get bogged down on this issue. This section is just a primer and laying the groundwork for the rest of the book.

The Book of Revelation indicates there will be a time period of three and a half years of "great tribulation" just before the return of Jesus. This is the time that the Beast will have full dominion over the earth. In Revelation 13:5, we read that the Beast "was given authority to continue for 42 months." For the math-challenged among us, that is 3.5 years. Revelation 11 also mentions a time of 42 months, as well as a timeframe of 1,260 days (which is 3.5 years assuming the biblical 360-day year, where each month has 30 days). Revelation 12:6 also states a time period of 1,260 days, and Revelation 12:14 uses the phrase "a time, and times, and half a time." Assuming a "time" is a year, this is a convoluted way of saying 3.5 years. This same language of "a time, times, and half a time" appears twice in the prophetic book of Daniel, both in Daniel 7:25 and Daniel 12:7. In Daniel 7:25, this refers to the Beast or Antichrist at the end of days. "And he shall speak pompous words against the Most High, shall persecute the saints of the Most High, and shall intend to change times and law. Then the saints will be given into his hand for a time, times, and half a time."

So the Bible is mostly clear that the Tribulation will last at least 3.5 years. Some suspect this is the full time of Tribulation. Others read the Book of Revelation chronologically. The Beast rises up to full dominion in Chapter 13 and reins for 3.5 years, this being coined the "Great Tribulation." But there are many trials and torments depicted as happening before this in Chapters 4-12.

There is an argument to be made that the Tribulation is a full seven years, with the first 3.5 years just a bad time of trials and torments, and the second 3.5 years the "Great Tribulation" under the rule of the Beast. I will briefly mention this interpretation but encourage the reader to "do their own research" for further clarification.

The explanation for a seven year Tribulation is rooted in the end-time prophecies in the Book of Daniel. As briefly mentioned earlier, there is a prophesied time known as "the Seventy Weeks of Daniel", where each week represents seven years. Many believe that 69 of these "weeks" (483 years) have been fulfilled from the mid 400s BC up through the death of Jesus. With Jesus' death, the Christian Church Age began and the timeline paused.

CHAPTER 6: THE TRIBULATION

The final seven years will occur after the Rapture (end of the Church Age) and forms the Tribulation. Daniel references an end-time event known as the "desolation of abomination." Jesus himself also directly references the prophet Daniel and this "desolation of abomination." It is understood to be a desecration and sacrilege of the Holy Temple in Jerusalem. Some evangelicals believe the Beast will literally live in Jerusalem for a time or travel there and desecrate either the Holy Temple or the site it previously stood on. Again, any interested reader is encouraged to further study up on the "70 Weeks of Daniel" and prophecy in general.

Without getting further bogged down, a quick summary seems prudent. Whether the Tribulation is seven years or half that time, the Bible is clear about one thing. A great "Beast", aided by the "false prophet", will rise to full dominion over the earth in the final days before the return of Jesus. It will be a time of great torment and suffering for those still alive on earth. That Beast is the Antichrist. It is time to talk about the Antichrist.

Chapter 7: The Antichrist is not Satan

The term "Antichrist" gets thrown about loosely these days. For church-goers, they have heard about the Antichrist countless times in sermons and bible studies and conversations with fellow believers. For non-Christians, the concept of the Antichrist is prevalent in pop culture. It was historically depicted in art and lore in medieval and Renaissance Europe. More recently, the Antichrist has been featured in books and movies and tv shows and Halloween costumes and everything in between. The word is recognized by all in pop culture at large and in the common vernacular generally. And yet, it seems the word and concept is completely misunderstood by most. The majority of people either think the Antichrist is the Devil/Satan himself or perhaps the son of Satan. Nothing could be further from the truth. To understand this book and the questions it poses, it is prudent to dispel this notion right off the bat. To repeat, the Antichrist is **NOT** the Devil and **NOT** the "Son of Satan." If a faithful believer or curious scholar is looking for Satan in the flesh, they will never spot him.

In pop culture and secular culture at large, the concept of the Antichrist comes from the Bible but doesn't let details get in the way. Movies like Rosemary's Baby or the Omen series have portrayed the Antichrist as either the Son of Satan (comparable to Jesus as the Son of God) or as a young, evil child who grows into a worldwide dictator with hellish intentions. In both cases, the Antichrist has ties to Satan and Satanism in general. It seems clear that this is the predominant view of The Antichrist writ large, as the term has become almost synonymous with Satan or the Devil. Many would view the Antichrist as the Devil in human flesh. The same attributes and symbols associated with Satan have been ascribed to the Antichrist - pentagrams, devil horns, the color red, hellfire flames, red eyes or pupils, a pitchfork, etc. Similarly, attributes of the Antichrist, mostly his number or mark 666, have been ascribed to Satan himself. The two are often used interchangeably. But the Bible paints a very different picture.

When one mentions end-times biblical prophecies, most people immediately think of the Book of Revelation and the Antichrist. It may surprise some, then, to learn that the word Antichrist does not appear in the book of Revelation. In fact, it only appears in the Bible four times, all in the books of the apostle John. The book of Revelation, also written by John, refers to the authoritarian ruler during the great Tribulation as the Beast. The book of II Thessalonians uses a different descriptor. In II Thessalonians chapter 2, the apostle Paul discusses the second coming of Jesus. Verse 2:3 states "Don't let anyone deceive you in any way, for that day will not come until the rebellion occurs and the *man of lawlessness* is revealed, the man doomed to destruction." As mentioned, the book of Revelation refers to the Antichrist or Man of Lawlessness as the Beast. As a reminder, Revelation 13 identifies two distinct beasts that will rise up and rule the world during the Great Tribulation. One of these is the Man of Lawlessness, the Antichrist. The other beast is coined as the "false prophet." He seems to be a "right-hand man" or enabler who helps facilitate the reign of the first beast.

Neither of these beasts is Satan. In Revelation 12:9, Satan is depicted as the red dragon. In the next chapter, the same dragon is characterized as a separate being from the two beasts. Satan gives power onto the first Beast, the Antichrist. He is a man who seems to have been healed of a mortal head wound (Revelation 13:3) and a man who speaks great things and blasphemies (verse 5).

Soon after in verse 11, the second beast is revealed. The key takeaway at this point is that neither beast is Satan. Furthermore, there are no verses that state or imply that they are offspring of Satan, possessed by Satan, or even worshippers or followers of Satan. It is clear that these men are not of God, or more accurately not of Christ. It follows, then, that they will be secular men of sin. All men are sinful, but some say these men may best symbolize the gateway sin that has tempted mankind for all time. As Timothy 6:10 instructs,"the love of money is the root of all evil."

A key goal of this book is to challenge the conventional wisdom and presuppositions of the term Antichrist. That nomenclature has just too much cultural history and stereotypes attached to it. As such, I will use all three terms interchangeably - the Beast, the Man of Lawlessness, and the Antichrist, with a preference for the first two. The term "Beast" is used in the book of Revelation in the most direct passages that describe the Great Tribulation. The term "man of lawlessness" is used in the books to the Thessalonians, which most vividly describe the Rapture of believers just before the great Tribulation. These terms, without the loaded Satanic imagery of "Antichrist," most accurately describe the man the Bible instructs us to keep watch for at the end of days.

Chapter 8: The False Prophet

The focal point of this book is about the Beast. But in Revelation chapter 13, the apostle John sees a second beast in his harrowing vision of the end times. What does the Bible say of this second beast?

While the first Beast (Antichrist) will be the authoritarian ruler of the world during the Tribulation for 42 months (Revelation 13:5), the second beast seems to be his enabler or right-hand man. In Revelation 13:12, we read that this second beast comes into prominence after the first, and that he exercises all the power of the first Beast. He will cause mankind to follow and worship the first Beast. In verse 13, we read that he does great wonders or marvels, even causing fire to come down from heaven in the sight of men. These great wonders or powers will deceive mankind into worshiping an "image" of the first Beast. In verse 15, this second beast has power to "give life" unto this image of the Antichrist. Verses 16-18 indicate it is this second beast that enforces or enables the "mark of the (first) Beast," a future required mark that duals as both a sign of loyalty and means for financial transactions. The mark of the Beast is analyzed in great detail in the next section.

In Revelation 19:20, this second beast is specifically described as the "false prophet that wrought miracles before him, with which he deceived them that had received the mark of the beast, and them that worshiped his image." This false prophet/second beast is ultimately cast alongside the first Beast/Antichrist into the lake of fire burning with brimstone.

The descriptions about this second beast have perplexed countless students of Biblical prophecy. At first glance, it sounds as if he will be a wizard or sorcerer, a magician with superpowers that defy logic. He makes fire come down from the heavens. He makes an image appear to come to life. Revelation 19 adds complexity to his character, identifying him as the false prophet. It seems he portrays the first Beast as the world's Savior/Messiah, and he causes all mankind to do the same, to worship the Antichrist. He is the "false prophet" because he promotes and facilitates the Beast, who is the false Christ.

Who is this false prophet? Who is this man who will empower and bring glory to the Beast? How will he do it? This will be fully explored in this book's explosive final section.

Chapter 9: Debunking the "Unholy Trinity"

You do not need to be Catholic or Christian to have heard of the Holy Trinity. But for some students of the Book of Revelation, there is an "unholy trinity." What is this phrase, and is it appropriate?

The Holy Trinity comes from the New Testament and refers to the concept of God in three persons - God the Father, Jesus the Son, and the Holy Spirit. God is found throughout the Bible and is the Creator, the singular spiritual being worthy of worship in the Old Testament. He is the God of Abraham, Isaac and Jacob, and he is the God of both Christianity and Judaism. The entirety of the New Testament (and indeed the literal meaning of 'new testament') concerns God coming to the earth in human flesh form. For Christians, this is Jesus Christ. God in heavenly God-form became known as God the Father, and God in earthly human-form became known as Jesus Christ, the Son of God. Jesus came to earth to sacrifice himself once and for all for any who believe. The "old testament" of sacrificing animals to God as an atonement for sin was replaced by this "new testament", Jesus sacrificing himself to atone for the sin of all mankind.

After Jesus's death and resurrection, he promised he would return to the earth again at the end of days. In the meantime though, Jesus instructed his disciples He would leave them with the Holy Spirit. The Holy Spirit is God in invisible, earthly spirit form and completes the Holy Trinity. Christians believe that they can be filled with the Holy Spirit, that it is the invisible force for goodness that roams the earth. The Holy Spirit can live in the hearts of man. For Christians, the Holy Spirit is the purported reason that Christianity spread historically out of the Holy Land

and throughout Europe, the Americas and beyond. Skeptics might claim that, at times, it was weaponry and brute force (the Crusades) and not the Holy Spirit at work. I digress.

Catholics use the concept of the Holy Trinity at the end of each prayer. They offer their prayers in the name of the Father, the Son, and the Holy Spirit (sometimes called the Holy Ghost). This is done while gesturing the symbol of a cross from their head to their waste to their shoulders. This concept of the Holy Trinity is steeped in Christian text and culture, but the sign of crossing oneself like a Catholic has permeated into pop culture at large. It is not uncommon to see even a non-believer mimic this action in a time of great stress or duress (sometimes for comedic effect).

In the prophetic Book of Revelation, there are three central figures portrayed as being opposed to the will of God and the Lord Jesus. The first is of course Satan aka the Devil, referred to in Revelation as the dragon. This is not an interpretation; the Book of Revelation clearly says the dragon is Satan (Revelation 12:9). The second is the Beast, introduced in Revelation 13. Again, this Beast (capital B) is the Man of Lawlessness or Antichrist. The third figure in Revelation is the second beast, also known as the "false prophet" (Revelation 19:20). The wording will get confusing, as there are two beasts. Throughout this book, I will simply refer to him as the second beast (lower-case b) or false prophet. The dragon will give power unto these two men, and they will influence mankind until the return of Jesus. But do they actually form an "unholy trinity"?

In one sense, I understand the moniker "unholy trinity." During the Tribulation, three key figures will be working against the will of God, against the model of Jesus, against the power of the Holy Spirit. We like to portray things as good versus evil, so it is easy to say three for this team versus the three for that team. Scripture tells us that the dragon (the Devil) will give power to and use these two men to do his work. The work of the Devil is to fool and deceive mankind away from God, Jesus, and the Holy Spirit. The work of the Devil has never been to cause man to worship him and become Satanists. The Devil has never been a self-promoter; he is rather an adversary to God, a fallen angel against the goodness of the Lord. Some say his greatest trick is to convince mankind he does not exist. How does the Devil work? He fools mankind, tempting all humanity into sin and all that which is not of God. Again, Scripture tells us the dragon will give power unto the two beasts, his two agents in the field. His agenda will be their agenda. What will their agenda be?

The first Beast, the Man of Lawlessness, will eventually rule or govern over mankind. During the Tribulation, he will come into full power and eventually be worshiped by the masses. This is discussed elsewhere in this book, but suffice to say that conditions for all on earth as the Tribulation begins will be so trying and horrible that a power void will ensue and a leader emerge. The Beast is that leader. His agenda will not be to convert humans into devil worshippers. His agenda will be sin and self-glory. The Bible tells us that the love of money is the root of all evil (Timothy 6:10). This man will likely love money (greed) and any other of the deadly sins. He will love things opposed to the salvation of our God through Jesus. He will cause others to love money as he does. He will lead others into his destructive ways of earthly riches and pleasures. His motivation will be to further enrich himself monetarily and in ego, power and vanity. He will demand complete and absolute loyalty, and by the end, this will transition into complete worship.

The second beast, the false prophet, will similarly work to guide humanity away from God. His figurative sermons and words may not be about spiritual matters; he could be a believer in worshiping humanity itself. This is the great trick of Satan, that God is not real, that Jesus is not real, that Satan himself is not real. The only thing real is the human world. Some say this second beast could be a poster-child for human innovation and reliance on oneself, absent of God. He may also love money and power like the first Beast. His inclusion in Scripture assures us he will have great utility and relevance. Curiously, he is described in Revelation 13:13 as performing "great signs, even causing fire to come down from heaven to the earth in full view of people." Specifically, he could enable the worldwide power of the first Beast through this innovation and technology, including this power to control fire between the heavens and the earth. But how could controlling fire between the heavens and earth help the Beast? Why exactly is this very specific, unique ability mentioned in Revelation? Again, this is explored in this book's explosive final section.

Ultimately, I do not like the moniker of the "unholy trinity." It carries with it too many assumptions and leaps to judgment. Specifically, one could incorrectly infer that the two beasts are Satan or the Devil in human form. This is not true. It is misleading and unhelpful. It further insinuates that the beasts will preach Satanism or forcefully preach against God directly. This also may not be true, at least in their rise to power and prominence. Again, the work of the Devil is not to directly attack God or preach against God. It is to deceive and tempt. Deceive and tempt. It follows that the two beasts will deceive and tempt mankind into their beliefs of salvation. For these beasts, salvation could be found through money, power, influence, fame, legacy, and all the earthly pleasures that are against the Word of God. They won't speak against God or Jesus, at least not initially. They will figuratively preach their lifestyles, their enriched ways of life.

But who are these men, and are they alive on earth today? It's time to consider that very question.

Section 3 -

The Beast

If you have made it this far into the book, congratulations! Those first two sections were necessary to lay the groundwork for what you are about to read. They contained a lot of information about God, Jesus, the Bible, and 'end times' prophecy. But most importantly, they established the timeframe and setting for the Beast's reign on earth. It is my hope that they have shed light on what millions of evangelical Christians have heard at church and bible studies for decades. Millions of us either believe a lot of what you just read, or we at least are familiar with some of it. For any evangelicals reading this book, I hope you will continue with an open mind. Our faith in God must be stronger than our devotion to any flawed men.

The first two sections of this book were mostly informational and explanatory. Much of the rest of this book will read a bit differently. This is the turning point. The rest of this book will seek to ask questions and explore possible answers. It is the work of years of intensive research, critical thinking, and analysis of world events big and small. What you are about to read in no way should be misconstrued as biblical truth or prophecy of any kind. What you are about to read is also not an accusation or allegation against any living person. Rather, it is an extension of the Constitutional right to freedom of religion. In America, any Christian has the freedom to worship and to verbalize their religious beliefs without retribution or retaliation.

THE BEAST

The next section is a long read, four chapters best read together in one sitting. Allow yourself ample time to read before continuing. It will be all about the Beast and the red-hatted politician. It will include an analysis of what the Beast's temperament and persona will be like. Does it match up to the persona of the bombastic billionaire? This section will also look at the history of famous people and leaders who were accused of being the Antichrist and just why speculation often surrounds any modern U.S. President. But most importantly and shockingly, it will delve deeply into the "mark of the Beast" and if that mark is already out there, hiding in plain sight. In a literal dramatic twist that flips this script upside down, every reader may already be familiar with this mark.

Chapter 10: The Beast's Traits

If I said facelift, you might think of the late Joan Rivers. If I said body augmentation, you might think of the Kardashians. If I said colored glasses, perhaps Elton John comes to mind. Mr. T is known for a mohawk, and Dolly Parton has big, ahem, hair. Napoleon was short, and Hitler had a short mustache. Many times, famous people become memorable because of a physical trait, or they add a signature physical trait to become more legendary. Either way, physical appearance matters to us humans. We always remember those who look unique and different. It stands to reason that in his ascension to power, the Antichrist may also have some distinct physical traits that make him unique and unforgettable.

Sadly, the Bible is vague on physical descriptors of the Antichrist. We could speculate that he will have a unique appearance or trait like the aforementioned celebrities, but it would be just that - speculation. We do know he will be a man, as he is referred to as the Man of Lawlessness or Man of Sin (depending on translation) in Scripture. He is also referred to as the Beast. Because he is a human man, he will not have cloven hooves or walk on all fours as a literal beast. He may, however, have an aura about him, a figurative beast or titan of the world. He may also have some sort of head wound that has healed (Revelation 13:3, Revelation 13:14). Other than that, the Scriptures are tight-lipped on his appearance.

The Antichrist will definitely have a unique, distinct personality. While the Bible does not give us the full-on Myers and Briggs personality test description of the Beast, we do get several hints and images. From there and with some good ole common sense, one can easily discern and extrapolate character traits of this future worldwide leader. To start and by definition, the Antichrist should (by the height of his reign) be someone against the Christ, or one posing as the Christ. He will be a wolf in sheep's clothing, or perhaps more accurately a Beast in Lamb's clothing. Spotting the phony or imposter is not always easy. But despite his best efforts, his true colors will always shine through.

As mentioned previously, the relevant biblical passages referring to the Beast (earth's last ruler just before Armageddon) are found in the Books of Daniel, Matthew, John, II Thessalonians, and Revelation. Daniel describes the last ruler in this way: "The king shall do according to his will" and "he shall exalt himself and magnify himself above every God." From this, we can surmise the Antichrist is both *highly self-serving* and *egotistical*. Also from the Book of Daniel, he "shall honor the god of fortresses instead of these…with gold and silver, with precious stones and costly gifts." This tells us the Antichrist will be extremely *materialistic*, a lover and ambassador of money, wealth, luxury, and excess. He might even literally have an ornate, opulent "fortress" directly on the sea.

The apostle Paul addresses the Antichrist in II Thessalonians 2, describing him as "the man of lawlessness" and "son of perdition, who opposes and exalts himself against every so-called god or object of worship…proclaiming himself to be God." From this, we know assuredly the Antichrist will make fantastic claims; he will be *boastful*. This goes hand-in hand with his egotistical nature. He will not just think highly of himself; he will make great claims of his authority and greatness, eventually likening himself to God or to Christ. As "the Man of Lawlessness" personified, the Beast will be *above the law* or consider himself above the law. He will commit atrocities that would destroy any other human, especially one aspiring to world domination. He will be a Houdini who escapes judgment and accountability in his rise to power.

In the Book of Revelation, two beasts emerge just before the end of times. Scholars and pastors and good Christian folk interpret these vague descriptors in many varied ways. It is generally accepted that one of these beasts is the worldwide authoritarian leader, the Antichrist. Any ruler always has a right-hand man, or enabler, and this will be the second beast's role. "Beast mode" never means timid, cautious, delicate, or compassionate. Rather, the use of the descriptor 'beast' tells us the Antichrist will be *fierce, ruthless, savage, aggressive,* and *deadly*. Yes, the Antichrist will be a figurative beast.

Perhaps the biggest clue as to the personality of the Antichrist is in the actual word, "antichrist." His personality and morality should be the opposite of Jesus Christ. What is the true nature of the Antichrist? We must first examine Christ himself. First and foremost, in the Bible, Jesus is the Son of God or God in human flesh form. We can deduce the Antichrist is *not of God*, meaning he is not a true believer of God the Father and Jesus the Savior. Jesus was the "Prince of Peace" and a healer (both figuratively as the spiritual bridge to God and literally as a physical healer.) We can thus know the Antichrist is not a man of peace and healing. He will be a *man of conflict*, a uniquely *divisive* leader. He may even be a literal anti-healer, an obstacle to those who promote healing (doctors, nurses, etc).

So many other attributes are associated with Jesus. Where Jesus was full of love, the Antichrist would be *hateful*. Where Jesus was forgiving and full of grace, the Antichrist would be *unforgiving* and *vengeful*. Where Jesus had compassion and mercy, the Antichrist would show *no empathy*. Where Jesus was obedient (to the will of God), the antichrist would again be lawless. Where Jesus was humble, the Antichrist would be a *braggart*. Where Jesus was "the way, the truth and the life" (John 14:6), the Antichrist would be a *liar*. He would be the greatest liar the world has ever seen. Nobody would lie as often or as fantastically as this man. To conceal himself, he must lie and lie often. He would lie about who he is and what he truly desires. He would be a convincing liar. He would have to be in order to fool the Church, the collective of those who claim to follow Jesus.

We will revisit these traits later in this section. But first, it's time to talk about the mark of the Beast. It's time to explore who was accused of being the Antichrist over the centuries. It's time to consider if perhaps, just perhaps, that mark is out there already, hiding in plain sight.

Chapter 11: The Mark of the Beast

The Book of Revelation is the dramatic final conclusion to the Bible, a cryptic, befuddling look into the future, a warning for believers and non-believers alike. In this Book, the apostle John, writing late in his life and many decades after the birth of Christ, documented his harrowing visions for the future of mankind. It builds upon and adds to prophecies found elsewhere in the Bible, particularly in the books of Daniel and Matthew and both books to the Thessalonians. It arguably contains the least literal and most puzzling excerpts in all the Bible. Scholars and clerics and preachers and laymen alike have interpreted the book in any number of ways for centuries. The study of Revelation reached a fever pitch in the late 20th century. With widespread speculation that the world could end with the new millennium, interest was at an all-time high. This was especially true in evangelical and fundamentalist Protestant churches. Indeed, thc study of the end times shaped my childhood and continued into adulthood. To this day, my parents still end conversations often with "Well, if we are even here in 5 years. The world may end before that." I have heard some version of that my entire life.

As analyzed extensively earlier in this book, many obsessed over the world ending exactly in the year 2000. In evangelical circles, interpretations like the Millennial Day Theory put a bullseye on the year 2000, as did the statehood of Israel in 1948 (the generation born then would see the return of Jesus). Other factors that led to the paranoia included the warp speed advancement of technology in the 20th century. This included the creation and proliferation of nuclear weapons. For the first time, man theoretically had the power to end the world, or at least kill off most life forms if a nuclear war broke out and led to a nuclear winter. Other biblical passages also sparked intrigue about the impending apocalypse, including Matthew 24 and its warning "of wars and rumors of wars" just before Christ's return. The biggest wars the world has ever seen occurred in the 20th century, including WW1 and WW2. The rumors of war seemed prophetically fulfilled with the Cold War and its threat of nuclear Armageddon. Of course, passages can be interpreted many ways, and the Bible is not always clear and direct like an IKEA instruction manual. Yes, decoding everything the Bible says about the end times is anything but straightforward.

Of all the symbolism and vagueness contained in the Book of Revelation, perhaps one passage composed of three verses has mystified mankind more than any other: Revelation 13:16-18. This is one of those passages that has transcended religious territory and entered the lexicon of pop culture at large. It is a passage that challenges the reader to use his or her brain and figure out the meaning. It teases that it is indeed possible to fully understand this symbolism. It is, of course, the passage referencing the name and mark and number of the beast, 666.

The Book of Revelation was written in Greek by the apostle John on the island of Patmos off the coast of Greece. I know these passages in English. Because I believe the Beast could be an English-speaking American, I will consider all possibilities about Revelation's symbolism and meaning, including that it was intended to be interpreted by English speakers at this exact time in history. I first studied the passage about the Beast's mark in the King James version of the Bible. Verse 16 seems to indicate that in the end times, after the great Beast comes to full power, there will be a requirement for "all, both small and great, rich and poor, free and bound, to receive a mark in their right hands, or in their foreheads." Verse 17 indicates "no man might buy or sell, save he that had the mark, or the name of the beast, or the number of his name." Verse 18 gives the final tantalizing challenge to the reader: "Here is wisdom. Let him that hath understanding count the number of the beast: for it is the number of a man, and his number is six hundred threescore and six." There it is, the riddle to end all riddles, the mystery of the mark of the Beast and his number, 666.

The number part has perplexed and intrigued clerics and theologians for centuries. Especially in the days of Christ and just after, some people considered a person's number as a code, with each letter of their name assigned a corresponding number (think 1 for "A", 2 for "B", etc). Rulers began to get assigned numbers historically (Henry the 5th, for example). In modern times, people have many sorts of numbers (social security number, telephone number, passport number, credit card numbers, etc.) Still, nowadays, we generally don't associate a person's name as having a corresponding number. It is unclear what the apostle John is referring to for the beast's number, or the number of his name. Did John simply add the Roman numbers of I, V, X, L, C and D together? Did he see the actual number written out?

Again, biblical translations are not perfect, and the Book of Revelation seems anything but literal. The New World Translation of these three verses reads slightly differently: "It puts under compulsion all people…that these should be marked **on** their right hand or **on** their forehead, and that nobody can buy or sell except a person having the mark, the name of the wild beast or the number of its name. This is where it calls for wisdom: Let the one who has insight calculate the number of the wild beast, for it is a man's number, and its number is 666."

CHAPTER 11: THE MARK OF THE BEAST

Imagining the Antichrist in our modern world requires an open mind, and in what follows I do not let exact semantics limit my thinking. After all, if spotting and identifying the mark of the Beast and the Beast's number were easy, it wouldn't require the "wisdom" and "understanding" that the apostle John describes in verse 18. Also of note, most theologians traditionally equate the Beast's mark and number (666) as the same, though the verses referenced above state otherwise. The wording of the King James Bible again is this: "And that no man might buy or sell, save he that had the mark, **or** the name of the beast, **or** the number of his name." It seems the beast's mark, name, and number are three separate things visually, and having any of the three on one's person (right hand or forehead) during the Beast's reign would suffice.

Interestingly, the Greek word "Xapayua" from John's original text translates most directly into "trademark" as opposed to "mark." Traditional translations of the Bible seem to have discounted that, as most men simply do not have a trademark. **Most men**.

Before attempting to decipher who could be and who cannot be the Beast, it feels prudent to discuss the Bible's authorship itself. For many Christians, especially Protestants, it is believed that God himself wrote the Bible through men - that the Holy Spirit inspired and guided the writing of each book of the Bible. This view is key in understanding how symbolism can be interpreted. As for the Beast's number, it is quite possible that the apostle John, filled with the Holy Spirit, recorded his visions in a manner to be best interpreted by the generation it applies to. In other words, if John saw the numerals 666 written in modern numeric form instead of Greek, he did not write "I saw three oddly-shaped circular marks I've never seen before". It is wholly possible that, through inspiration of the Holy Spirit, John recorded what he saw through the lens of the people who it applied to - namely, the people alive during the end times. Many scholars and clerics disagree and insist that it was written just for the churches and believers in John's day circa 50-70 A.D. But this narrow view could render the entire Bible as obsolete and only meant for people alive thousands of years ago.

I believe that end times prophecy, inspired by the Holy Spirit, was recorded to be best interpreted by those alive at the end times. It is a crude map for those alive just before the return of Jesus. It serves little purpose to be written only for people who died thousands of years before the prophecies are fulfilled. As such, it is quite possible that the apostle John saw the numbers 666 in modern numeric form. Perhaps that is even what is meant by "wisdom" and "he who has understanding" or "he who has insight." Perhaps only those who recognize 666 in modern numeric form have the necessary understanding. The people in John's day did not have this insight. It was not written for them. But whose mark is it? Who could be the Beast?

Over the centuries, any number of world rulers and even organizations have been accused or offered up as the possible Antichrist, and wild justifications have been given as evidence. Perhaps the first was Nero, a Roman Emperor who persecuted the Church from 54-68 AD, the same time that John wrote the book of Revelation. Nero was the emperor during the First Roman-Jewish War which led to the destruction of the Second Temple in Jerusalem, the Temple of Jesus' day. This was speculated to be the "desolation of abomination" prophesied by Daniel and Jesus. But the world did not end after Nero's death, so he could not be the Beast of Revelation.

By the early Middle Ages, some began to falsely label certain Catholic popes or the papacy collectively as the Antichrist. This grew out of the rivalry between Reformists and Catholics, with some early popes referring to themselves as the Vicars of Christ, or substitutes for Christ. The Catholic tradition of marking foreheads with ashes at Lent, which began in the 8th or 9th century AD, may not have helped, given the reference to forehead marks in Revelation 13:16. By this time, many came to see the mark of the Beast and the Beast's number (666) as the same. One could humorously envision a random ashen mark somewhere must have inadvertently resembled three 6s, not unlike how people purport to see Jesus' or the Virgin Mary's likeness in a random shadow or piece of food. To be clear, no Pope has been the Beast of Revelation.

Later in the Middle Ages and into modern times, it became common for opponents of powerful rulers to label their adversary the Antichrist. Historical figures considered as the possible Antichrist included the Russian czar Peter the Great, and by the 20th century any host of world leaders, such as Benito Mussolini, Joseph Stalin or Adolf Hitler. The atrocities Hitler committed against the Jewish people, God's "chosen people" biblically, lent credence to this theory.

History is interesting, but alas none of these people can be considered the Antichrist/Beast, because the world still exists, Jesus has not returned, and these rulers are dead. It is clear from Scripture that the Antichrist, the great Beast, will come into full power during the Great Tribulation just before the return of Christ and the end of the world as we know it. The Beast will not simply die and then the world goes back to normal. As such, he is either still to come in the future, or he is out there now.

By the 1980's, the age of modern conspiracy theories really took off in America. Who killed JFK? Was there really a moon landing? Are green aliens hidden in Area 51?? Millions pondered the unknown and unexplained every week with host Robert Stack on NBC's Unsolved Mysteries. In evangelical circles, theories about the Antichrist and impending doom reached a fever pitch too. The newest candidates labeled as the Antichrist included Mikhail Gorbachev and Ronald Reagan. If the world was indeed to end around the year 2000, it made sense for a current world leader to be the Beast, still consolidating his power before establishing a new world order. The evidence and rationale was always sketchy and sometimes humorous, but such is the case when the Bible leaves such cryptic clues begging for misinterpretation.

President Ronald Wilson Reagan was the leader of the 20th century's newest superpower, and he had a nuclear button at his fingertips. He could destroy large swaths of the earth or start WW3 with one rash decision. Oh, and his first, middle, and last name had six letters each: 666. Yes, decades before Q'Anon, people speculated. On the flip side of the Cold War, you had the Russian President Gorbachev, a communist leader with similar nuclear capabilities. The peculiar, distinct red birthmark on the top of his balding head was interpreted by some as THE mark of the Beast. Of course, in the end, these two played nice and altered world history in a surprising turn toward peace and freedom, a far cry from the apocalyptic scenarios feared during the Cold War.

In the 1990's, the evangelical Protestant leaders in America and their faithful flock became even more closely aligned with the Republican party and its appeals toward the "moral majority." In this environment, the newest Democratic American leader became a candidate for Antichrist. But President William Clinton didn't fully fit the "bill." He was a little too folksy sounding and perhaps more interested in chasing interns than truly establishing a new world order. As such, it was his wife, shrewd and sharp, that was seen by some as the "brains and bitch" of the operation. From then on, some speculated maybe Hilary herself was the Antichrist. Decades later, millions still obsess that she is evil incarnate, and a newcomer on the political scene in 2016 won over evangelical christians in part by simply playing on their disdain for her.

But first, still in the 1990's, new theories began to take hold in evangelical circles concerning the Beast's mark. Rather than focusing on the number 666, the discussion shifted to the passages about the right hand and the mark being used to purchase goods. Speculation came to center on new microchips and barcodes that were revolutionizing modern life. Some were even being implanted into pets so they could be tracked if lost. Was this the mark of the Beast? As referenced earlier, if you ever walked through a Tribulation House in the 1990s, created by evangelical churches and similar to Halloween walk-through haunts (only churchier), you are familiar with this theory. To this day, many evangelicals are convinced that this is the eventual mark of the Beast. Technology has indeed made it possible that a human could buy and sell goods by swiping their (implanted) right hand. This theory made it tougher to pre-identify a candidate for Antichrist, as any leader could use this technology and make it their mark after they came into power.

As theories go, this one about rfid microchips was progressive in its logic, applying the modern world's technology as a practical means for prophecy to be fulfilled. This satisfies the practicality of how a mark would be needed to purchase goods and why it would be near impossible to refuse the mark. You either swipe your rfid chip at checkout, or you go hungry. If taken literally, this mark could potentially be designed to resemble 666 or some other symbol unique to the Antichrist. Yes, I was warned in many a "Tribulation House" not to take the mark of the Beast. "The end is near, do not let them implant your hand!"

As the year 2000 approached, a new threat came from the technology sector. A crisis began to emerge in the computing space. Our modern world was changing rapidly in the computer age. Things that had once been recorded in books and ledgers were now being stored in computers. Experts began to raise red flags about the impending century and millennial change. This came to be known as the Y2K crisis. It seems the dates and calendars loaded into computers of this time had flaws and errors. Without intervention and a fix, computers could and would interpret the new century/millenium as the year 1900 or even 1000 instead of 2000. It was feared chaos would ensue. Bank accounts and holdings could be erased or deleted overnight. Financial institutions and world stock markets could freeze or collapse. The energy grid or power plants, including nuclear facilities, could be paralyzed or disabled. The list of fears went on and on. Millions believed that the end was near, that the year 2000 was indeed doomsday. And yet, the ball dropped in Times Square, Sting's "Brand New Day" rang out on all the tv coverage, and human life continued on unscathed.

With the passing of the year 2000, the fizzling of the Y2K crisis, and the continuation of the world past this millennial change, end times speculation hit a speed bump. Was the timeline slightly off and the end still nigh, or should good Christians stop obsessing and get on with their lives? The events of September 11, 2001 changed everything. A new threat to world peace and the general world order presented itself that day with unimaginable force. Terrorism took center stage, the "War on Terror" began (wars and rumors of wars, again), and evangelicals had a new candidate for the Beast - Osama bin Laden. He was ruthless, evil, and as a militant Muslim, he was seemingly opposed to Christ and a natural enemy of both Christians and the Jewish people. The "War on Terror" meant that the U.S. became embroiled in Middle East conflicts in Iraq and Afghanistan. Instability and fighting in the Middle East always seems to lead to speculation about prophecies and the return of Jesus. But bin Laden never asserted worldwide dominance. More importantly, he is now dead so cannot be the Antichrist. Nevertheless, with all the terror threats and Middle East conflicts and anthrax scares during this time, my parents kept warning me, more than ever, that Jesus was returning soon.

With the advent of around-the-clock partisan cable news and satellite radio shows and podcasts in America over the last two decades, an extreme fracturing and political polarization has occurred. As such, it was inevitable that some would label Barack Hussein Obama the Antichrist. His name being of Islamic origin was justification enough for many. Sadly, his race (the first black American President) was also proof enough to some bigots that he was evil. Obama also presided during 2012, when fears about the end of the Mayan calendar stoked paranoia about impending Armageddon. The 2012 prophecies never materialized, but they did give us an entertaining film starring John Cusack.

It seems certain every American President moving forward

will indeed garner speculation on whether he or she is the great final Beast. No one man wields as much power, nuclear or otherwise, as the American President. Arguably, no other country currently impacts the global fate of mankind more than America. The American dollar is the global reserve currency. The United States' military may be the strongest and most visible and active worldwide. The USA has the most advanced nuclear capabilities. In terms of language and culture, much of the globe has become much more "Western-ized" over the last few decades, or more accurately "American-ized". One could imagine that if aliens landed on earth and said "take me to your leader", no one person would fit that role as much as the American President. So yes, it is very natural and believable to consider that the eventual Antichrist could be the most powerful man on earth, the President of the United States.

In the last few years, a political outsider stunned the masses and rose to great prominence, seemingly out of nowhere. He had fortune and fame for decades, but his thirst for power was new. He was known as a rich playboy, a man from great wealth who ran casinos and beauty pageants and owned opulent buildings and mansions, ornate with gold-plated furnishings. Some say above all else, he loved money. He loved money and he loved himself. He promoted himself and his brand endlessly. His name was plastered on all his properties. Inexplicably, this alleged adulterous New Yorker with an alleged unfiltered haughty and crude tongue (Revelation 13:5-8) won over Protestant Christians quite quickly.

He didn't go to church regularly or seem to know anything basic about the Bible. He claimed the Bible was his favorite book, but he wouldn't or couldn't recite a single verse when pressed.

And yet, many in the Church believed his every word, that he was indeed one of them. He even told them he was being persecuted because of his strong Christian faith (that was why his taxes were under perpetual audit).

As President, he began to upset the established world order. He threatened and insulted nuclear dictators, then would praise and celebrate them. He alienated peaceful allies and hosted and praised adversaries instead. Some say he sowed distrust in everything that wasn't him, distrust in truth itself. Some say this man seemed to have his own agenda, an agenda with himself as the center. He was indeed a curious leader, unlike any ever seen. That so many millions of evangelical Christians were allegedly deceived by this man caused some to ponder: is this the Beast? Is this how he hides in plain sight? Are the very people who study and obsess over end times prophecy so hypnotized under this man's spell that they don't see him for who he is?

There are endless theories about the mark of the Beast and the number 666. Before examining and revealing the literal mark (a noun), it is important to consider the **act** of accepting the mark of the Beast. During the Tribulation, all humans will be required to accept the mark to buy or sell. It could be just as simple as saying "I accept the mark" or wearing the mark. Or more grimly, humans might be lined up like the children and youth in the Hunger Games reaping, forced to take the mark. Or maybe, just maybe, with great linguistic irony, it begins by actively marking (verb) a mark, that this action will set in motion the prophetic rise of the Antichrist into full power.

It seems curious that the beast's number is just the number 6 repeated exactly three times. The use and symbolism of the number three, or things happening three times, is found throughout the biblical scriptures. Of course, Christ is part of the holy trinity, God in three persons - God the Father, Jesus the Son, and the Holy Spirit. It seems fitting then that the Anti-Christ would also have a relation to the number three. Accepting the AntiChrist, or taking his mark, seems to be a denial of the real Christ. Biblically, the disciple Peter did just this, denied Christ. To save himself from persecution just before Jesus was crucified, Peter denied that he knew Jesus three times - three times before the cock crowed, just as Jesus warned him would happen (Matthew 26:34, Mark 14:30, Luke 22:34, John 13:38). Peter swore he wouldn't and was on guard not to do this, and yet he did it anyway. His spirit was willing but his flesh was weak. He denied Jesus three times. Is this how modern man will first choose the Antichrist himself and take his mark? Will they choose him three times, choose a (some say) morally bankrupt ungodly man as their earthly savior and leader, choose him with unwavering fervor and passion usually reserved for deities?

If you can't defeat conspiracy theories, join them. At the time of publishing, one well-known man is currently running for President a third time. Many people will mark his name for a third time in 2024. He was born in the sixth month. His first name has six letters and begins with a D, just as 666 written in Roman numerals is six letters long beginning with a D (DCLXVI). This man says he has done more for Christianity than anyone else ever (presumably even Christ for whom Christianity is derived.) He called himself the Chosen One while looking up to the heavens. Polls show his followers trust him to tell the truth more than they trust their own families or their religious leaders. Could this be the marking of the Beast? Could this directly correlate to the disciple Peter's denial of Jesus three times before the cock crowed? Is a vote for a President, a literal mark on paper, the act that finalizes the Beast's power? Presidents usually serve a max of two terms, so it is very rare to see a man's name 3 times on the final general ballot. And yet here we are, on the cusp of millions of people, even millions of evangelical Christians, about to "mark" a man's name for the third and final time - a man, some say, whose very fiber and morality seems ever so anti-Christ-like. A lot of people are asking - will Christians still figuratively worship this man, despite his atrocities? Does his return to power lead to the authoritative New World Order and Tribulation?

Most clerics and theologians believe that the mark of the Beast is an actual mark - a visible symbol such as a tattoo, birthmark, logo, trademark, etc. A wonderful illustration of this exists in pop culture. In the Harry Potter franchise, author J.K. Rowling used clear biblical imagery in her treatment of the powerful villain Voldemort. Voldemort had serpentine features and a sidekick snake to boot. He was evil personified, and his look and imagery was meant to evoke that evil. His features and stylings were in line with how humans have imagined Satan for centuries, serpentine like the Devil himself in the Garden of Eden. But more relevant, Voldemort had a symbol, a clear logo or trademark that embodied his essence, his brand. The mark was a skull with a python-like snake coiling down underneath. His followers were called Death Eaters, and they each had this mark on their forearm just above the hand (sound familiar?) Anyone who had that mark, Voldemort's mark, was a known follower of the "Dark Lord." Nobody else had this mark unless they had devout loyalty to Voldemort. The mark was distinct and easily recognized and understood to all characters in the fictitious wizarding world. Yes, J.K. Rowling's imagery clearly aligned with modern interpretations and renderings of the Antichrist and the mark of the Beast.

Of note, this fictional mark of Voldemort seemed to be voluntary at first. However (spoiler alert), after Voldemort thought he had killed Harry Potter, he attempted to assert supreme and absolute power. He gave ALL magical wizards and witches a choice - follow him and convert to the dark side or be killed. Presumably, any new convert would have received the death eaters' mark in his/her forearm shortly thereafter, but Neville Longbottom intervened before we found out. At any rate, this parallels exactly with the understanding of the mark of the Beast in Revelation. Once the Beast's reign comes to full fruition and he has unchallenged power over the earth, all would presumably either take the mark or face persecution, hunger, and death. To escape spiritual damnation during the Tribulation, one would have to summon the courage of Neville Longbottom and resist the mark and conversion to the dark side. To be clear, at the time of publishing, the reign of the Beast has not begun yet. We may, however, be in the phase where his mark is already out there, albeit on a voluntary basis for now.

In our modern world, trademarks and logos and symbols are everywhere. Some are easily recognized and identified by humans worldwide. Most anyone could see a certain swoosh mark and know it represents Nike. The golden arches 'M' clearly means McDonald's. Some marks are powerful enough to conjure up more than just recognition. A tiny horse with a mounted polo player can convey not just the brand Polo Ralph Lauren, but indeed the lifestyle or socioeconomic status of anyone who wears it. The same could be true of the Mercedes-Benz three-pointed star inside a circle. Symbols that are this well-known and powerful in their interpretation are usually associated with companies or business entities. It is exceedingly rare, however, for a world leader to be known by a symbol. One could theoretically associate a leader with his nation's flag, but that would not separate him from all the other leaders who had held power in that same nation. As referenced earlier, the literal Greek translation of Revelation 13:17 includes the word for "trademark", not "mark."

One world leader did have a very distinct mark or logo. As mentioned, Adolf Hitler was a prime candidate to be the Antichrist nearly a century ago. At the height of his reign, his significance far outweighed just being the leader, or furor, of Germany. His power and influence affected the global masses (World War II), none so more than the Jews. An estimated 6 million Jewish people (God's chosen people) were murdered by the Nazis at Hitler's behest, killed in gas chambers. Millions more soldiers and civilians (including an estimated 7 million Russian civilians, many Jewish) died at the hands of Adolf Hitler.

While Hitler had a distinct mustache, his "mark" was clearly the Nazi symbol, the swastika. Most anyone can visualize the swastika (a plus sign with lines extending to the right at each of the four ends). More importantly, most anyone has an immediate association with what the symbol means. Anyone who brandished the symbol was clearly telling the world they were loyal to Hitler and the Nazi movement, and their world-views aligned with his. At a basic level, this included the belief in a hierarchy of races, that Aryans (white people of northern European descent) were the superior race, and that the Jewish people were a dirty, inferior people. In today's world, a person wearing or adorning a swastika likewise aims to convey that they are anti-Semitic and believe in white supremacy. The most devout neo-Nazis still envision a world where the Jewish faith and heritage is eradicated, that all Jews are murdered into extinction. Hitler wanted this and personified evil itself. Very few, if any, world leaders have had a symbol as powerful or well-known as Hitler's swastika. If Hitler had been the Antichrist, one could envision this Nazi symbol forced on the right hand or forehead of every human during the Tribulation and the reign of the Beast. Hitler died in April of 1945.

Though Hitler was not the Antichrist, his horrifying acts and legacy may have set Biblical prophecy in motion. As referenced earlier, the statehood of Israel (and of the Jews, God's chosen people) is often interpreted as a sign of the end times. Israel became a state/nation on May 14, 1948 - not long after the Holocaust and World War II. Some interpret prophecy to indicate the generation born at Israel's rebirth would see the end of days (Matthew 24:32-35). It follows that the Beast may very well have been born at this time as well, he himself a part of that generation. One thing is clear - if anyone of that generation born in the late 1940's is indeed to live to see the return of Christ, time is running out very quickly.

As mentioned previously, a major public figure born in 1946 just before Israel's rebirth is running for the office of American president for a third time. As it turns out, this man also has a very well-known trademark or symbol or slogan. His trademark also has an abbreviated form. He has been about personal branding his entire life. Most recently, he sells red hats and other gifts and memorabilia adorned with his name or this trademark or its abbreviation. He also seeks to profit from selling altered Bibles at $60 a pop, but I digress. Just hearing the four letter abbreviation pronounced like a word, most anyone knows who it refers to and what it conveys. People wear hats and shirts with his name or this signature logo to show their support and devotion toward this man. The most hardcore of his legions of fans have been described by some as cult-like, their association with his movement defining their very identities. Some of his followers seem to almost worship him, his rallies evoking the passion and fervor of a religious revival. Some see him as a modern-day savior of America and defend his every action and utterance, no matter how allegedly offensive or untrue or treasonous. A lot of people say he redefines truth for his followers with his alternative facts. They cling to his every word and rise to action when he asks. He convinces supporters that crimes are not crimes, that rejecting law and order is ok, as long as it is in his name to benefit him.

Thousands committed felonies and stormed the U.S. Capitol in his name on January 6, 2021. They risked their lives and freedom for him (does any other human inspire such devout passion towards himself?) All the while, they flew flags with both his name and his trademark or its abbreviation. More interestingly, they wore hats with his name or trademark or its abbreviation. A hat's markings are on the front and generally rest over a person's forehead. Yes, his devout followers already wear his name or mark or abbreviation on their foreheads.

It seems prudent to reiterate that according to Scripture, the "mark of the Beast" during the Tribulation could be any one of three things: the Beast's name, the Beast's mark or trademark, or the number 666. The mark will be required to buy or sell goods. It will be present on a person's forehead or on their right hand.

The Beast is not currently in full worldwide power. We are not yet living in the Great Tribulation. Credit cards and cash may be required to buy and sell goods, but marks of a person's name or trademark slogan or number are not.

CHAPTER 11: THE MARK OF THE BEAST

But is the writing on the proverbial wall, or in this case, on millions of foreheads already? Are the pieces of the puzzle starting to come into place? Are more and more clues staring us in the face? And what about that curious number, 666? And what about the future mark on the right hand? It's time to turn our thinking upside down.

Chapter 12: The Upside-Down

If you've ever watched a horror movie with religious or demonic undertones, you've likely seen the symbol of an upside-down cross. Inverted crosses appear in countless horror flicks, including The Conjuring, Paranormal Activity, The Amityville Horror, and Rosemary's Baby. In The Nun, the crosses all turn upside down just before an effective jump scare. The imagery needs little explanation. Whereas a normal cross is a symbol for Jesus Christ, an upside-down cross is understood as imagery for Satan, demons, or simply evil in general. The symbol could easily apply to the Antichrist as well.

Fans of "Stranger Things" on Netflix know all about a different 'upside-down'. It is a world that mirrors our reality closely, but things are askew. It is darker and more bleak. It is a dreary place where reality is twisted and distorted. It is a place where sinister forces lurk, where shadowy figures operate and thrive. As evil forces in the 'upside-down' begin to disrupt life on earth, the misfit protagonist kids slowly figure it all out. To learn the truth and save the world, they eventually cross over into the 'upside-down' underneath their town of Hawkins, Indiana and fight evil head on.

For any astute reader, you may have seen a lot of headlines in 2024 about upside-down American flags. It turns out some proponents of the red-hatted politician have begun to fly their flags upside down. Historically, this gesture was only used by sailors of U.S. military vessels in distress, a kind of maritime SOS. But during the 20th century, protesters on all sides of the political spectrum would occasionally incorporate inverted flags to further their cause. Again, most recently and visibly, it has been adopted by the most ardent supporters of the red-hatted politician. Some flew upside-down flags during the insurrection of January 6, 2021 as they stormed the nation's Capitol. Many have flown them at their homes this way, including a conservative Supreme Court Justice. It is coming to symbolize the same thing as all those red hats.

In the last chapter, those red hats were discussed. Currently, they are just that, hats. People wear hats to show support for their sports teams all the time. People wear hats with a brand's logo on them frequently. True, these politician's red hats carry more weight - they clearly signal a political or cultural ideology. They can be especially divisive. But, to be clear, they are not required to be worn by any authority. They are not required to make purchases. At the time of publishing, they are not the literal mark of the Beast. But those hats are curious. They almost always have either the man's name or his trademark slogan.

His slogan or trademark or symbol is of course Make America Great Again. The abbreviation is four capital letters, MAGA. This abbreviation, pronounced as a word, is used worldwide to describe him, his supporters, and his political and cultural movement and ideology. The four letters are as much a symbol as a word. They speak volumes. No other world leader in recorded history has actively tried to monetize and sell his own brand like this - indeed, millions of people have purchased and currently own MAGA merchandise, usually those hats.

Of interest and importance which will become clear shortly, perhaps no other leader has been associated with capital letters like this man. Yes, his symbol and slogan MAGA is capitalized, but it doesn't stop there. Before his political ascent, his trademark was simply his name. It was adorned on his properties and skyscrapers, and it utilized only capital letters. He never used lower-case letters. As a leader and influencer, this man speaks to his followers regularly via the internet and Twitter (now X) or a competitor of Twitter, Truth Social, which he created. He became well-known for ranting in all capital-lettered posts (internet code for shouting). Indeed, if a Family Feud writer surveyed 100 people with the question "Name a famous person who types in capital letters", one could envision this man ranking #1. But what if the seemingly innocent and excessive life-long use of capital letters has had a more nefarious, specific purpose all along? What if the use of capital letters has kept hidden the crucial piece of the puzzle of Revelation?

I generally do not like conspiracy theories. They are often baseless or without merit or perhaps based on a rumor. They are often the work of an overactive imagination, an attempt to discredit reality, an attempt to justify one's own biases and world-view, an attempt to distort or jumble the truth. I am hard-wired to think like a prosecutor. I prefer hard evidence and proof. I prefer unimpeachable, absolute truth.

It is with great hesitance that this book must at times venture into the conspiracy theory unknown, to think like an end times Q'anon dabbler. And yet, that is the reality for any who seek to spot the Beast before it is too late. The Bible is just too cryptic with many of its descriptions of the last days. To even be a faithful Christian, one must suspend what we can see with our own eyes and believe in an unseen God. We must pray to an invisible presence that we've never visually seen or audibly heard. I am a born-again Christian and I believe in Biblical prophecy. With great pause, I must take you into the figurative "upside down", only literally.

CHAPTER 12: THE UPSIDE-DOWN

To repeat, what if the seemingly innocent and excessive life-long use of capital letters by the red-hatted politician has had a more nefarious, specific purpose all along? What if the use of capital letters has kept hidden the crucial piece of the puzzle of Revelation? What if MAGA was typed in lower-case? What if we view it from a different angle, say upside-down.

666w

Turn your book or screen upside down and see it for yourself. It is just maga written upside down, the lower-case 'a's with elongated stems. Is this what the apostle John saw in his vision, in the nightmarish dream that he wrote as the Book of Revelation? Did he actually see the lower-cased MAGA symbol written upside-down? Did he see 666w?

There is a lot to unpack here. First, this is not an accusation, merely a hypothetical question as pertains to my Christian faith. Second, if true, why would the apostle John see 666w? What would the purpose be? Third, how would one explain the w next to 666? Let's unpack it all. With no rationale or reasoning, a conspiracy theory is just that, a theory. It only starts to gain traction if you corroborate with other evidence and rationale.

Why would the apostle John see a 666? Recall from Revelation 13:16-18 that the "mark of the Beast" is prophesied to be required on the forehead or the right hand to buy and sell goods. It seems like there is a clear dual purpose in this mark -

loyalty and money. The mark can be three things - the Beast's name, his trademark, or his number.

The name and trademark thing seems like a loyalty declaration. We see that now on all those red hats - loyalty and brand awareness. It is either an ironic coincidence or a prophesied truth, as some of those red hats say a name, and the others say a trademark four word slogan. Again, we see all this now already on people's foreheads, in that baseball-style caps feature writing that rests directly over one's forehead.

So what are we missing? The right hand may correspond with the number 666. In the future, the 666 part must be about the money. When you control a person's money and finances, you control them. My hunch is it will be the mark eventually required on the right hand. Financial transactions will likely not take place on the forehead.

What would a 666 on the right hand look like, and how would it relate to financial transactions? There are many possibilities - tattoo, handstamp, or perhaps a visible rfid chip or barcode. Or, just maybe, it could be something we know and see already, something much less invasive and not a violation of one's body. It could be a smartwatch.

In the 21st century, for the first time ever in human history, people can pay with their hands/wrist via their smartwatch. Currently, the most common logo on a smartwatch is a piece of fruit, an Apple. Given the role of the apple in the Garden of Eden, this could just be a coincidence or maybe a clever biblical clue (Tom Hanks in The Davinci Code anyone?) In the very near future, there could be any number of brands of smartwatches. The red-hatted politician (or a future ally) may even sell one himself one day, the same way he created his own social media platform to rival Twitter.

Imagine the watch worn on the wrist has a brand name on its edge, exactly where the wrist ends and hand begins. Imagine that brand name is lowercase maga. From a first-person standpoint, one could look down at their own hand and read "*maga*". If, in his vision, the apostle John saw lower-case "maga" on a person's hand, he could theoretically have seen "maga" from one direction. But he wouldn't have seen this because he was not looking down at his own hand. Instead, he would have seen it upside down and the "*666w*" from a different angle, the view he would have standing across from a person.

Under this hypothetical, it is possible to believe people could initially take the mark without even realizing it is the mark of the Beast. "It's just a brand of watch." If the mark simply said 666, it would be obvious. The number 666 is too ingrained in our collective psyches and pop culture at large. This could be how and why even some Christians who know prophecy inside-out could still be fooled. Luckily, at the time of writing, they still have time to remove these trademarks from their wardrobe. They still have time to not buy or adorn any future smartwatch with a maga logo on it. These marks are not required to purchase goods…yet.

Let it sink in that the Antichrist or great Beast of Revelation 13 will have a trademark - a trademark that will seemingly be very famous and well-known. Most men don't have a trademark, but the Beast will. Everyone would theoretically know it like the back of their hand, literally, as it would be required to buy or sell goods. They would know and recognize the trademark, the name, or the abbreviation instantly. It follows then that the Antichrist will be extremely well-known too, perhaps the most famous person alive on earth. Again, if a Family Feud survey asked "Name the most famous person alive on earth", who might likely be the number 1 answer at this very moment in time? Only a man of great status and power and fame could commandeer the moniker of "Beast."

And what about that w next to 666. What is it? Again, this is all wild speculation that would not hold up in a court of law, and under this hypothetical it doesn't really matter. If I had to speculate, I could think of several things. The w could stand for wisdom (Revelation 13:18), as in it takes wisdom and understanding to decipher it. Or perhaps it is a sideways 3. Three things represent the Beast - his name, his trademark, and his number. What else could a 3 represent? This could be why the apostle John used the word "three-score" in verbalizing six hundred and sixty-six. Or, a sideways three could be the fitting link to Peter's denial of Christ three times. A sideways 3 could also be described as the number 3 lying down dead, as in the Beast reigns and the Holy trinity (God in 3 persons) is perceived as dead.

Alas, this is all just speculation, that maga written upside-down resembles 666. Many will deem it ridiculous, absurd speculation. I pray it is. I am self-aware enough to admit it seems wildly imaginative. At the same time, it is also wildly coincidental. What are the odds, especially as the MAGA crowd has taken a liking to turning things upside-down themselves? Again, it would not hold up in a court of law. It is not meant to. But what if? What if? God forbid any of us find ourselves alive during the Great Tribulation. But if we do, I will not under any circumstance wear a watch or mark with any iteration of 666.

CHAPTER 12: THE UPSIDE-DOWN

> Critical update July 2024 - during final edits for this book, a stunning development occurred and demands attention. This chapter was first written in early 2023 and later edited to mention upside-down flags. The idea of turning MAGA upside-down to see 666w may seem conspiratorial and crazy. It did to me too. It no longer does in any way. It turns out that on his official campaign merchandise store, the red-hatted politician is now selling new hats that feature his name written upside-down! What are the actual odds? Perform your internet searches for proof then continue reading below.

But just because the world's most famous, boastful, and potentially powerful man has a trademark that, when viewed upside down, resembles the Beast's number - that doesn't prove anything. It's surely just a coincidence. End times stuff will involve the Middle East, specifically Israel and the Temple. And this man has no interest in anything related to the Middle East, right? He is not at all drawn to all that money and wealth in the Arab world, right? He would never want a skyscraper (with his name adorned on it) built in Jerusalem, right? And sure, this man sent his Jewish son-in-law (with no official foreign relations experience) to the Holy Land to broker peace, and yes this man believes he has done more for Jews and Christians than any human ever, but that doesn't mean anything either, does it? Except that son-in-law, curiously sent to broker Middle East peace (while also earning billions in a deal with the Arabs), had other endeavors as well.

It turns out nearly two decades ago (at time of publishing), in the strangest of coincidences that defies belief, that same family member and advisor purchased a prominent New York City skyscraper on the west side of glitzy 5th Ave. Would you believe the address, 666 5th Ave. As it was on the west side of Manhattan, the address could also be typed as 666 W 5th. The Beast's number right there plain as day. What are the odds? Jesus Christ lived an impoverished life, drawn not to riches and earthly desires, but rather embodying the message of love and selflessness. Surely then the Antichrist will pursue and represent the exact opposite - a life completely centered around riches and self-glory.

The Antichrist will figuratively turn Christ's teachings upside-down in every way. So once again, we must literally view things upside-down.

666w 5th

Examining 666 w 5th upside down, we see "4⸸5 maga". We know who 45 is, as in the 45th President. We see MAGA again, and we can clearly see an upside-down cross. If Christ is represented by the cross, then who might that upside-down cross refer to?

It is for the reader to decide if this is an even wilder, one-in-a-billion coincidence. It is for the reader to decide if it is worth the risk of one's eternal soul to wear this man's name, trademark, or upside-down abbreviation on one's forehead or right hand or wrist. It is for the reader to decide if it is worth the risk to mark his name on a ballot a third time.

This book is not a trial or accusation. But if it were, this trial would have more than one exhibit of "evidence." This book is about more than one peculiar conspiracy theory. It's about looking at everything as a whole with as much knowledge and information and insight to decide if there is something to all of this. Earlier in this section, we looked at likely qualities of the Beast of Revelation. It's time to revisit those same descriptors and traits in this added context - do they apply to the red-hatted politician?

Chapter 13: The Beast's Traits Revisited

We know the Beast will be a literal world leader, destined to rule the entire world during the Great Tribulation. He could be a current leader, or someone about to come into power. He may have already been in power and so remains influential, his shadow hovering over all current events. Perhaps he is soon to regain that power or even expand it. The question is simple - do the traits of the Beast from Scripture match those of the red-hatted politician? Does it seem like it fits like a glove, or is it nothing like him at all? It is for the reader to decide.

Earlier in this book, various physical and personality traits of the Antichrist were considered. Again, there is not much to go on biblically as far as appearance. This author speculated that the Beast could have a very distinct trait that contributes to his fame. It is for the reader to decide if that quality fits the red-hatted politician. Could you see his shadow or hairstyle and know who it is? Is he that famous and unique-looking?

The Bible (Revelation 13:3) cryptically indicates the Beast may have some sort of mortal head wound that has healed. It is unclear what is meant here, whether the wound is literal or symbolic. Perhaps this will become clear in the future.

> Critical update: On July 13, 2024, as this book was nearing final publishing, an event of epic proportions rocked the world. There was an assassination attempt on the life of the red-hatted politician at a campaign rally in rural Pennsylvania. A gunman with an AR-15 opened fire and struck the ear of this politician. He survived within an inch of his life, literally, as a bullet to the brain would have been fatal. An innocent attendee was less fortunate, shot and killed as he shielded his family.

> This author and this book do not condone political violence or violence of any kind. God is the ultimate judge, not man. Attempted murder is amoral sin, period. No person should read this or any book and become radicalized in this manner. Again, this author condemns this brazen act in the strongest terms.
>
> Still, the prophetic significance of this horrific event is compelling. In Revelation 13:3, the Beast is described as having had a mortal head wound that was healed. From this, people marveled at the Beast and followed him. It is for the reader to decide if this is yet another remarkable coincidence or something else entirely.

Luckily, the Bible does give us several clues about the personality and demeanor of the Beast, as outlined in chapter 10. It seems prudent to revisit those traits and consider if they apply to the red-hatted politician.

Self-serving: a self-serving leader would act erratically, unpredictably and seemingly devoid of principle. He would make decisions based on how it affects him, his power, his wealth, his status, his agenda. This leader would quite likely conflict and quarrel with his own advisors, confounding his closest allies as his self-interest always comes first. He would try to surround himself with "yes men", those who go along with his every whim and desire. If his motives are questioned or agenda stalled, he would fire them.

Egotistical: an egotistical leader would consider himself the greatest man alive. He would be the most amazing ever at everything, in his own mind. He would describe himself as a genius, an expert on everything. A lack of credentials or experience would not slow him down.

Boastful: From his own mouth, nobody would be as great a leader in the history of leaders, believe him. He would make fantastic claims. It would not matter if they were true; facts would not slow him down. Moreover, he would have others make fantastic claims about him, even if they were provable falsehoods. This leader would know the masses are attracted to confidence, and he would be endlessly, boastfully confident come hell or high water.

Materialistic: this leader would love money and luxury. He might even be a symbol of wealth and excess, of the endless, unapologetic pursuit of earthly treasures. If Robin Leach still hosted "Lifestyles of the Rich and Famous", this man might be a recurring star of the show. Perhaps he was before his ascent to power. He would use his newfound power to gain more wealth. He would profit from his power in self-serving ways no leader ever had before. It would defy logic. He might even defraud the very subjects he presided over. He would try to conceal that fraud. He would claim he had nothing to hide, all the while paying lawyers millions to hide it all.

Above the law: this leader would be lawless. It is why the Beast is also known as the Man of Lawlessness. He wouldn't just bend the rules or escape judgment or accountability, he would actively work to reshape the law in all ways. He would mold who enforces it, and he would shift how the population views it. He might even claim he could commit a felony in cold blood and not lose any support. He might claim he is immune from prosecution. Not all are immune, just him - his opponents should be imprisoned. Over time, his followers would acquiesce. A double standard would apply. He would be able to do anything and everything and it would be dismissed and disregarded by his followers. They would make excuses or look the other way, all in their minds for the greater good. This trait is essential. It is how the Antichrist will fool even the Church. People will marvel at how this one person defies conventional wisdom. Where others fall, he always rises from the ashes unscathed and more powerful.

Fierce/savage/ruthless: again, this leader is described as a beast in Revelation. A beast is never timid and does not back down. He would have a tongue (spoken words) like a snake, vapid and quick-striking. If any person challenged him on any issue, no matter how small or petty, this beast would pounce in words and actions. Even the powerful would come to fear him and his ferocity. Nobody would want to get on his bad side or attract his ire. He would be savage, even to the weakest and most downtrodden in society. By attacking and villainizing the weak and ostracized, he would further cement his power with the masses. Jesus would welcome and lift up the poor, the meek, the orphan, the prisoner, the stranger. This man would do the opposite. As the end of days drew nearer, this leader's aggressive ferocity could destabilize the world. He could attack other leaders, leading to economic hardships and wars or rumors of wars. These things must come to pass, and the Antichrist could be the one stoking the flames of the fire.

Not of God: this leader would not be a follower or believer of Jesus or God. He would not ask God for forgiveness, for he would not need forgiveness (in his own mind). He would believe in himself and convince the masses to worship him. They may not worship him at first, but if he offered what they needed, they would come around. As a deceiver, he could give the appearance of being a Christian as needed. It would be an act. He would only be spotted acting Christian when cameras were around or it was needed to coalesce his power. He would use and fool the Church. He would also happily take money from good God-fearing Christians. Over time, some of them would divert money they gave to missionaries and the needy and give it to this wealthy deceiver instead. He would be so convincing, that even if he were a billionaire, he would convince working-class Christians to donate more money to him.

Divisive: this man would conquer and divide. He would divide people over everything in his ascent to world domination. Chaos and a mistrust of societal staples could be essential to establishing a new world order just before the end of days. This leader would divide opinion on everything. Only he is to be trusted, certainly not anyone who goes against him: the media, the clergy, other leaders, the military, the police, certain judges. Anybody who goes against him would be vilified. Families would be divided, neighbors would fight, friendships would end - all because of this man's divisive words, rhetoric, and actions. A new world order can only come to exist once the bedrocks of society and norms have been destroyed. His followers will come to distrust the system and reality itself - they will believe him and only him.

Hateful: this leader would have a hateful heart. He would be like no other leader, in terms of his earthly relationships. All of his bonds would not be made out of love; rather, every relationship would be transactional. It would always be all about him and what he gets out of it. He would demand loyalty to himself, but provide it to nobody. A true sign of a hateful heart is how a person treats animals. This leader would likely have no interest in even the friendliest of animals, such as a dog. If an animal cannot further his power or wealth, then they have no purpose. His romantic relationships would not be based in love; they would be rooted in superficial and self-serving objectives. He would love the adoration from his followers but privately be repulsed by them. At Christmastime, a time of joy, peace, and love, he might show his true colors. Because the spirit of Christmas goes against his moral fiber, it would not be surprising if he issued vile, vengeful, hateful messages to the masses on Christmas Day year after year. This spirit of hate on Christmas Day from a so-called Christian would be unlike anything ever seen before.

Vengeful: A true sign of the Beast is his thirst for vengeance. He would always come after and attack his opponents or anyone who dared cross him - the rich and poor, the powerful and weak, the healthy or sick. He would exact his revenge against any and all. His vengeance would be shocking. Nobody would be off limits, even if they were a war hero or physically handicapped. If policemen defied his will, they would be expendable too.

No empathy: the authoritarian leader would have no capacity for empathy. He would see himself as above everyone else and unable to relate to the real-world strife and struggles of 'lesser' men and women. Before his final ascent to full domination, he could first be called on to act in situations that all leaders encounter - responding to troubles and tragedies to those who he leads. An empathetic person responds to emergencies and crises with compassion and aid. This leader would not. He would threaten to withhold help from those in need. He would lecture and degrade others in their most vulnerable times of despair. He might be gracious enough to callously throw emergency supplies to those who have lost everything.

Liar: this leader would lie repeatedly and unashamedly. It would be truly remarkable, the sheer volume and numbers of lies. If anyone went against him, he would lie about them. His followers would believe his every word, or come to believe every word. He would repeat lies enough times that people believed them as truth. His allies would lie for him. When called out on the nature of the lies, they would create new names for lying. Falsehoods would become alternative facts. This leader would lie about anything and everything to protect himself and further harness his power. Just as Satan is the great deceiver, so too will the Antichrist be a masterful liar. When caught in lies, he would pivot and deflect. His bait and switch tactics would be like a magician with smoke and mirrors, confusing the masses on what is real and true.

Above all things, Jesus was without sin. As God in the flesh, he came to earth to save mankind. He sacrificed himself. He replaced the animal sacrifices of the Old Testament, one final perfect sacrifice for eternity, the sacrifice of the Lamb of God - innocent, blameless, without sin. That is the core tenet of Christianity. The Bible verse John 3:16 may be cliche, ingrained in American culture by street peddlers with cardboard costume signage or sports fans with posters. Still, it encapsulates Christianity in one verse: "For God so loved the world, he sent his only begotten Son, that whosoever believeth in him shall not perish, but have everlasting life." If Jesus is the spotless Lamb of God without sin, the Antichrist is a lover of sin. He himself is sinful, and he encourages others to be sinful as well. By being over-the-top unapologetically sinful, he will cause even the faithful followers of Christ to fall away, enticed by the things he relishes. He will normalize sin and change people without them even knowing they have changed. They will love him and adore him, sin and all.

What sins will truly define the Beast? We know Jesus is life, eternal life for those who believe. In contrast, the Beast is death, eternal death and damnation for those who follow him and take his mark, the mark of the Beast. The Beast will appear in modern times, just before the end of days. In modern times, there are seven deadly sins.

The movie "Se7en" was released in theaters in 1995, just before the world was feared to end in 2000. Brad Pitt, Morgan Freeman, and Kevin Spacey dramatically burrowed the seven deadly sins into a generation's collective minds. All sins flow forth from these seven characteristics. It follows that the Beast will epitomize these seven deadly traits quite obviously for any and all to see, a poster child for these seven. The seven deadly sins: envy, gluttony, greed, lust, pride, sloth, and wrath. Is there a powerful world figure who embodies so completely all seven of these traits?

Each of the seven deadly sins will be addressed below. The examples next to each are hypotheticals, not allegations.

Envy - The Beast will be an envious man. He will want what others have. This could manifest in many ways, big and small. He will have to be better than others. If he plays golf, he will cheat to score better. If less people attend his inauguration, he will lie to say it was the biggest ever. If his wife gets older, he will trade her in for a newer model. If the newer model gained weight during pregnancy, he might cheat on her with a porn star. If a pandemic broke out and a cute little old man led press conferences, the Beast would get envious and insist on leading the televised updates himself. He would be so envious, he would vilify the old scientist. If anyone else stole the show in any way, he would vilify them with childish names. If a black man became president, he would insist he was illegitimate, a non-American.

Gluttony - The Beast will be overweight. He will literally be gluttonous when it comes to food. He may possibly have an affinity for fast food. Gluttony applies to more than just food, however. It is a general overindulgence in everything. He will be gluttonous for luxury and excess, a poster child for it. Nothing will ever be enough to crave his desires. Even if he has it all - money, power, fame, supermodel wife, successful kids, mansions, skyscrapers - he will want more.

Greed - similar to gluttony but more specific, greed refers to the love of money. The Beast will love money like no other. Much of his life will be about acquiring more money than anybody else. He will have opulent mansions and bigger-than-life skyscrapers. He will have toilets made out of gold. The Bible warns us that "the love of money is the root of all evil" (I Timothy 6:10).

Lust - the Beast will be lustful in every way. He will be well known for his sexual escapades, no matter how scandalous. He will lust after supermodels and beautiful women in general. He might speak of his own attractive daughter in sexual terms. He could have been a close associate of the late Jeffrey Epstein. He may have visited the Epstein compound. He could be a sexual predator who brags about groping women by their private parts. He would likely have extramarital affairs. He could be a rapist. He might even run and fund beauty pageants, afforded the unchallenged ability to walk into the changing rooms and view the contestants naked. He might even be accused of doing this at the Miss Teen USA pageant, where underage girls are undressed backstage. There might even be video or audio recordings of him talking about much of this.

Pride - the Beast would be very proud. He would be proud of himself and the things he has done. He would even be proud of things he has never done, proud that he could lie about it. He may call himself a genius. He would be endlessly confident in himself, too proud to know his deficiencies. He would be so proud of his name and brand, he would want it plastered everywhere on most anything. He would be too proud to ever admit defeat.

Sloth - this is the only deadly sin whose definition isn't as widely known as the others. Sloth refers to laziness, apathy, or lack of work ethic. The Beast may not be sloth-ful when it comes to things he wants (money, power, fame), but he would demonstrate sloth in other areas. If he were President, he may show a poor work ethic despite the high stakes. He might play golf rather than educate himself on world events. He might zone out during briefings with advisors and experts. He might have a slew of former advisors and allies sounding the alarm that he is unfit for office, that he lacks the attention span or temperament to lead.

Wrath - above all things, the Beast will have a thirst for vengeance. He will go after anyone and anything that challenges him. He will delight in ruining people who speak poorly of him. He will threaten people. He will enlist others to attack his enemies. He will instill fear in others, both friend and foe. His propensity for wrath will help him consolidate power. Even the powerful will acquiesce to his every demand. He will make once mighty officials look like cowering children. His wrath will be so palpable, he will change the world. During the Great Tribulation, the Beast will demand full loyalty. Failure to take his mark will result in persecution. Any candidate to be the Beast must show a fundamental propensity towards wrath. He must be the type to demand absolute loyalty or else.

Again, it is for the reader to decide if any of the above traits fit the red-hatted politician. It is for the reader to decide if the hypothetical prosecution is starting to bolster its case, if a bunch of circumstantial evidence compounded together is starting to make a lot of sense.

Section 4 -

The Deceiver and the Dictator

At the time of publishing, we are not living in the prophesied Great Tribulation, yet. As such, the Beast has not ascended to his prophesied status as a global dictator, yet. But assuredly, there are specific signs to look for. The Antichrist will be a masterful deceiver. Sure enough, in the key end times prophecies found in the Bible, believers in Christ are warned repeatedly about being deceived. If someone could possibly be the Beast of Revelation, they will most assuredly fool even the faithful. As such, it is essential now to transition to the subject of the Christian faith (and faithful) as it relates to the red-hatted politician.

In legal speak, this fourth section will look at the opportunity and motives of the red-hatted politician. It will first consider the Book of Revelation's clear biblical admonition to all people, including Christians. Are they being warned about the bombastic billionaire? It will then explore the red-hatted politician's relationship to Christianity. Are his previous words and actions those of an actual Christian, or is he the prophesied wolf in sheep's clothing? Lastly, it will examine the red-hatted politician's current agenda and future plans. Do his words and actions come across as a soon-to-be dictator who demands absolute loyalty? Does he have any motives to rule as a dictator? And most shockingly, is he being worshiped and heralded as the new Messiah?

Chapter 14: The Conspicuous Warning

"He that hath an ear, let him hear." This important phrase is used eight different times in the book of Revelation. Amid all the symbolism and confusion of John's visions in his final apocalyptic writings, this warning at first glance seems straightforward and clear. The Word of God is beseeching and pleading that anyone who reads or hears these recorded words pays attention. The phrase emphasizes the importance of the passages that directly precede it. It conveys that the words and admonitions are intended to endure until the very end. They are not just intended for the apostle John's contemporaries or fellow Christians alive at that time; they are intended for all people to come. But is there a deeper meaning and significance to when and where the phrase is used? Is it a specific warning for Christians about being fooled by the Beast?

"He that hath an ear, let him hear." Again, some version of this admonition is used eight different times in the book of Revelation. The first seven uses occur in chapters two and three. As discussed previously, these chapters occur in the days of John, just before he is whisked away "in the spirit" to see what is to come. John writes seven short letters to seven different church locales in his day. He addresses the state of affairs of each church. To put it bluntly, he (as instructed by God) tells each church what it is doing right and wrong. I believe that the Holy Bible is the Word of God inspired by the Holy Spirit. As such, there must be a clear reason why these two chapters are included in the Book of Revelation. It seems obvious that they are meant for Christians and believers in all times, not just John's present day. Additionally, it can be reasonably interpreted that the warnings and admonitions apply to Christians who are alive at the end of days just before the return of Jesus. It is important to see what present-day Christians are warned about. After that, the all-important and oft-overlooked eighth use of the phrase in Revelation 13 will be explored.

Revelation 2:1-7 - To the church in Ephesus, John praises the Christians for their patience and good deeds and works. These works include identifying and trying false apostles, exposing them as liars. But then they are alerted that they have "left thy first love." They are instructed to repent and do their "first works." The verses can be interpreted many ways. In general terms, it seems they are instructed to stay focused on the Lord Jesus and his teachings. Their works should follow suit (worship God, feed the homeless, love thy neighbor?) But since this is included in Revelation, is there a deeper message for those Christians alive just before the end of days? Have they begun to be led astray by false prophets and "left thy first love" which is the Lord Jesus?

The verses hit me personally. They remind me of my grandparents and parents, who maintained their faith in Jesus despite all the "false apostles" that scammed them. They selflessly gave money to preachers and tele-evangelists and organizations devoted to harvesting souls for Jesus. Some were legitimate; others were not. My family donated generously to tele-evangelist Jim Bakker and his Heritage USA (PTL) ministry and vacation spot in the Carolinas. Bakker was eventually convicted for crimes related to misusing donations from faithful Christians. Some of the money was used as intended, while millions in donations he kept for personal gain or used to silence his secretary from exposing their sexual affair. He got busted for paying hush money for sexual indiscretion. Sound familiar? It seems at the end of days, there will be false prophets and phony influential “apostles” who are liars. If my grandparents were still alive, would they fall for any other ambitious public figures currently fundraising as devout Christians anointed by God? Would they again donate to a charismatic personality who silences sexual partners with hush money?

The other six churches that John writes to in chapters 2 and 3 are praised and rebuked for various reasons. They are commended for things such as their works, their patience, their poverty, their suffering, their faith, their charity, their holding true to the Lord’s name, etc. They are warned about idolatry, sexual sin, maintaining faith, false teachings, and riches and comfort. With each address, John concludes with “He that hath and ear, let him hear.” Those Christians that heed his words shall “ eat from the tree of life” and live with the Lord forever. Those Christians that repent and overcome and keep watch for the Lord Jesus shall be rewarded in heaven. Those that do not shall be cast out into eternal death. We know these words are directed towards Christians specifically, as John addressed the letters to the Church directly. It is of special note that those in poverty are praised (Revelation 2:9), and those relishing in riches and comfort are rebuked (Revelation 3:17). It would seem unwise for any modern-day Christians to praise and exalt any billionaires and seek the same earthly riches. The Word of God in Revelation is very, very clear. He that hath an ear.

It turns out that the phrase is curiously used an eighth time in Revelation chapter 13, the key chapter set during the Great Tribulation where we learn of the two beasts and the mark of the Beast. The beginning of chapter 13 details the emergence of the first Beast during the great Tribulation. The Beast, or Man of

Lawlessness, is revealed, and he arrives as a man of great wonders to all those still alive on earth, a man who garners praise and worship (verse 4). He speaks great blasphemies and boasts and comes into full worldwide power for 42 months, or 3.5 years (verse 5). It is prophesied that he will make war "with the saints" and gather power over all people of all nations (verse 7). In verse 8, it is prophesied that all men whose name is not in the Book of Life will worship him. In verse 9, we read "If any man hath an ear, let him hear."

The book of Revelation can be interpreted any which way, and I do not intend to add to its words. This is my analysis and mine alone, not the Word of God. I believe verse 9 is clearly included as a warning to Christians. It is intentionally out of place, as by this point in the vision the Church has been raptured away. It seems certain some who call themself Christian will not actually be raptured away and spared from the Great Tribulation. Some will still walk the earth when the Beast comes into full power. Scripture tells us others will, against all odds, accept the Lord Jesus into their hearts and convert during the Tribulation. In both ways, verse 9 draws a line in the sand for believers still on earth, that you either accept and follow the Beast or you worship God the Father and Jesus, not both. This is the last chance. It emphatically implies that Christians will be fooled by the Beast, hence the warnings. Christians will be fooled by his haughty, blasphemous tongue and wondrous cult of personality and power.

"He that hath and ear" is like a loud siren for the Church, the collective body of believers. The warning lights are flashing that a great deceiver is on the scene. It seems clear that he is or will be a wolf in sheep's clothing who deceives the very elect (Matthew 24:24). It seems intuitive that the apostle John is not warning

Christians about an obvious adversary; we are instructed to keep watch and not fall for the one who hides among us, one who only claims to love the Lord Jesus and love the Word of God, one who lies. We know how the serpent Satan tempted Adam and Eve in the Garden of Eden. He pretended to be friendly and promised them earthly treasure and bliss. He lied. The great Beast will do the same. He will first fool the Christians. This provides cover and will allow events to play out as prophesied. Any who speak against him will be dismissed. They would be called things like thugs or Christians in name only (CINOs?). It would just be a witch hunt. He that hath an ear.

> Update: I wrote this chapter in the fall of 2023. As the book nears publishing, yet again I am floored by the headlines and must add in an edit. It seems in Tim Alberta's new book "The Kingdom, the Power, and the Glory: American Evangelicals in an Age of Extremism", he recounts events from the presidential primaries in 2016. Specifically, the red-hatted politician was losing the Iowa caucuses to Ted Cruz, a self-identified evangelical Christian. After losing key endorsements from evangelical leaders and trailing in the polls (he finished third in Iowa), it is reported that he lashed out. Alberta details that a Republican official from Iowa was told by the red-hatted politician: "You know, these so-called Christians hanging around with Ted are some real pieces of shit." It should give every Christian reader pause to know that in his mind, the reality and veracity of someone's Christian faith is only as good as their loyalty to him. Endorse someone else? Fake Christian! Time will tell if he adopts the moniker CINOs as mentioned above. He has already stated that Jews who do not vote for him "hate Israel'' and "hate their religion", essentially calling them fake Jews.

It is also curious that this phrase “he that hath an ear” is used directly after the passages about the first Beast, who is the Man of Lawlessness or Antichrist. It is not used after details about the false prophet are given later in Revelation 13. Again, this drives home the point that Christians will support the Beast, that they are fooled by his words and supposed actions. We know the Man of Lawlessness will have a cult of personality; that is the only way to achieve worldwide power and control. Christians will unwittingly help him to his ascent to full power. The Bible is screaming for them not to be deceived, but some will be.

It follows then that the false prophet, the right-hand man or enabler to the ruling Beast, will possibly not be a self-described Christian or have such a massive following among evangelicals. The key Christian warning “he that hath an ear” is not included for this second beast.

To summarize, the key use of the phrase “He that hath an ear, let him hear” is a loud warning to everyone, including Christians. Its repetitive use in Revelation 2 and 3 tells us it is a code phrase for “This is important, listen up!” Its curious use in Revelation 13, just after the Beast is revealed, is another clear message. The Beast will fool Christians and use that authority to further his agenda. The Beast will not appear as a Satanist or dirty drug-dealing thug or unkempt murderer or a crazy person. He will look poised and polished and fool the very elect. Unfortunately, some say evangelical Christians today are indeed being deceived, unable to tell the difference between a true man of faith versus one who comes in sheep’s clothing.

Chapter 15: The Beast in Lamb's Clothing

In attempting to answer the question that sits on the cover of this book, one jarring thing kept nagging at me more than anything else. Sure, this man has a problem with the truth. He makes things up or stretches the truth. When proven to be incorrect, he often doubles down and repeats untruths ad nauseum. He changes the narrative and truth itself by convincing his supporters that everything else they hear is false - that only he tells them the truth. He lies about everything from his net wealth, property values, taxes, crowd sizes, poll numbers, weight, etc. But of all the whoppers he told, it was the ones concerning his faith that stood out. The moment he claimed to be a "strong Christian" is the first time I truly asked myself "Is He?"

To be clear, the Bible warns us not to judge others lest we ourselves be judged (Matthew 7:1). In the end, only God the Father is worthy to judge all of mankind. However, in the same chapter, Jesus (the sinless Lamb of God) also warns us to keep watch for false prophets (Matthew 7:15), which come to us in sheep's clothing but are actually ravenous wolves. It is in this spirit that I approach this subject not to judge others for their faith but rather to call a spade an obvious spade. If we see a blasphemous false prophet, are we not to speak out? Is this a ravenous wolf in sheep's clothing? Is he the Beast in Lamb's clothing?

The red-hatted politician was born into a Presbyterian household. Until he ran for President, this seems to have been the only connection this man had to anything to do with Christianity. In his adult life, there is no mention or record of him attending church services with any sort of regularity. In his thousands of pre-politician interviews, he never offered that he was a man of Christian faith or any details about this. His wives and children, also famous, never hinted at this. His employees, attorneys, friends, associates - there are no detailed accounts of his Christian faith from any of these people. Nothing about his life would give any indication that his love of Jesus was his driving force. His faith didn't lead him to reportedly associate with the mob, to run beauty pageants (and walk freely into the dressing rooms), to build casinos, to have affairs with porn stars, to swindle investors and students out of money, to sexually assault a woman inside a department store dressing room, to brag about using his fame to touch women's private parts. Nothing about his life screamed "I'm a super Christian!" And that alone is ok. Billions of people are not Christians. That doesn't make one the Beast.

The pretend metamorphosis occurred conveniently as soon as he announced his run for the American presidency. By running as a conservative, his only path to nomination was through tens of millions of evangelical Christian voters registered as Republican. He was initially trailing in the primary polls to a self-professed evangelical Christian. On the campaign trail in the South and Midwest, he began for the first time claiming the Bible was his favorite book. In an interview on Bloomberg network's "With All Due Respect", the following exchange occurred:

> Host - "You mentioned the Bible, you've been talking about how it's your favorite book... I'm wondering what one or two of your most favorite Bible verses are and why."
>
> Subject - "Well, I wouldn't want to get into it because to me that's very personal..."
>
> Host - "There's no verse that means a lot to you that you think about or cite?"

> Subject - "Well, the whole Bible means a lot to me but I don't want to get into specifics."
>
> Host - "Even to cite a verse that you like?"
>
> Subject - "No, I don't want to do that."
>
> Host #2 - "Are you an Old Testament guy or a New Testament guy?"
>
> Subject - "Probablyyyyy (hesitating) equal. I just think it's an incredible, the whole Bible is an incredible, I joke very much so they always hold up 'The Art of the Deal', I say my second favorite book of all time. But, uh, I just think the Bible is just something very special."

To be clear, any Christian asked his favorite Bible verse could answer more proficiently, as could many non-Believers. Most Americans who have never been to a church could easily lie "John 3:16" just from seeing sports competitions or sidewalk preachers. And yet, this man answered the question as if he had been asked how quantum physics works - he was completely stumped in every way about the contents of his self-professed "favorite book." It goes without saying that a Christian is probably a "New Testament guy", as the whole faith of Christianity centers around Christ - his life on earth and his sacrificing his life to save us of our sins. Jesus Christ only appears in the New Testament, and indeed the term "new testament" refers to the replacement of the old ways of sacrificing animals to God for atonement. Jesus was the final sacrifice for all mankind - the slain Lamb who washed away the stain of sin and made man white as snow again in the eyes of God. To be a Christian is to accept Christ and this new testament.

In the fall of 2015, the early leader from the Iowa caucuses was a self-professed evangelical, Ted Cruz. Suffering defeat to Cruz in the Iowa caucuses, the red-hatted politician seemingly stepped up his devout faith overnight. Moments after a televised debate, he was interviewed by CNN. When asked why his taxes were under audit by the IRS (a debate topic), he had the audacity to claim it was because he was such a strong Christian. I will never forget watching that moment live, and the video is easily found through internet search. It was a record screech moment. Would people actually believe this statement, such a bizarre attempt at pandering for votes? I am a Christian and my taxes have never been audited. Of course, taxes get audited because of omissions, errors, fraud - not religious affiliation. The red-hatted politician was found civilly guilty in New York for just that - financial fraud. But according to him, he was only audited for being super churchy. Over the next few weeks, to my surprise, the evangelical voters began supporting this man in higher numbers. His tactic was working. He was now just like them, a common God-fearing man allegedly persecuted for his faith.

In January of 2016, this newly devout politician traveled to Liberty University, founded by Reverend Jerry Fallwell and synonymous with evangelical education and culture. He was courting the southern Baptists and Protestant Christians in general. In his address, he cited "Two Corinthians 3:17, that's the whole ballgame…Is that the one you like?" He referenced this simply because it had the word 'liberty' in the verse and he was at Liberty University. Genius. More memorably, he verbalized the book of the Bible incorrectly, saying "two Corinthians" instead of "second Corinthians." This bizarre verbal gaffe again exposed he seemingly had no verifiable connection to the Bible or Christianity or church in any meaningful way, certainly not in the way he was portraying himself. First-graders in Sunday school know it is pronounced "second Corinthians." Regardless, his popularity with Christians inexplicably continued to grow.

CHAPTER 15: THE BEAST IN LAMB'S CLOTHING

In the fall of 2016 just before the election, a sex scandal captured the world's attention. This man, masquerading as a strong Christian, was caught on tape describing how he likes to sexually grab women in the genital region, and they let him do it because he is a famous star. I thought for sure his proverbial ship was about to sink. Evangelical voters had always been harsh and righteous against any politician who was adulterous or who fornicated or gave the appearance of any sexual sin, much less possible sexual assault. This conviction was a bedrock of the "moral majority." Indeed, the moral majority was outraged that Bill Clinton, as president, received oral sex from a White House intern - to them, an unforgivable, impeachable act of fornication and adultery. If an act of consensual sexual indiscretion was impeachable, how much worse was admitting to possibly sexually assaulting women against their will?

After the Access Hollywood tape was aired world-wide, I remember a religious Republican congressman from Utah stunned, declaring in an interview he could no longer vote for this man. He had a wife and kids and had to be able to look them in the eye with a clear conscience. After all, a vote for an adulterer or sexual deviant was unacceptable. I thought most moral Christians would follow suit. How could the born again in Christ support a self-professed sexual predator? To my surprise, this man didn't lose their collective support. My fellow evangelical Christians overwhelmingly selected him as their next President. They reasoned out that he was still the better choice, that God used flawed men throughout the Bible to advance his will. This loyalty to someone who does not really represent their morals and faith has largely stayed intact today.

Of course, pretending to be someone for votes does not make

one the great Beast of Revelation. Indeed, many politicians on both sides of the aisle are considered to be slimy, smarmy, baby-kissing phonies. Politics and corruption go hand in hand. The field is awash in power and money, and many men and women have either pursued politics in search of these, or have succumbed to the temptation. In layman's terms, a lying politician is hardly a concern for an impending apocalypse…or is it?

The President of the United States is arguably the most powerful man on earth. To see a man become that powerful by pretending to be a super Christian was alarming. Just after his election, two biblical verses came to mind. Again, Matthew 7:15 warns us to "beware of false prophets, which come to you in sheep's clothing, but inwardly they are ravenous wolves." I also pondered Thessalonians 2:3-4 "Let no one deceive you in any way. For that day will not come, unless the rebellion comes first, and the man of lawlessness is revealed, the son of destruction, who opposes and exalts himself against every so-called god or object of worship, so that he takes his seat in the temple of God, proclaiming himself to be God." This verse actually comforted me. The new President sure was boastful and sure did stretch the truth, but he did not claim to be God. He did not seem to be actually interested in issues found in prophecy - issues involving Israel or the Jews or the temple in Jerusalem or any of that. Sure, he was interested in women and money and power and fame, that's all. In that sense, the part of me attuned to apocalyptic matters was relieved. He wasn't the man of lawlessness who exalts himself, right?

It seems important to again mention a key nugget of biblical prophecy. It is the "desolation of abomination." This prophecy is first mentioned in the Book of Daniel. Jesus Christ himself also references this prophecy as a sign at the end of days that his return is imminent. This "desolation" relates exactly to the verse from I Thessalonians referenced in the preceding paragraph. During the Tribulation, the Beast will exalt himself in the "Temple of God." This is believed to be in Jerusalem where the Holy Temple stood during the life of Jesus. The Second Temple was destroyed in AD 70. The location was on the Temple Mount in Jerusalem. Today, this is where one finds the Wailing Wall (the only remaining piece of the Temple not destroyed), as well as the Dome of the Rock and the al-Aqsa Mosque. The prophesied "desolation" will be the Beast, at this site, proclaiming himself worthy of worship by all mankind. Because the Temple no longer stands there, it will either be rebuilt somehow (it is a contentious piece of real estate) or the desolation will occur in some other manner. (The Bible is unclear if building a skyscraper at or near this holiest of holy sites, complete with gold furnishings and your name on it, would count as blasphemy. To date, no man has attempted to do this. But I digress.)

The true turning point in how some viewed this man came later during his first presidency. He began to say things and to message himself in different ways, in ways that transcended politics. His reign as a President began to cross paths with issues of Biblical Scripture and prophecy. He was no longer just masquerading as a super Christian for votes and appearances. Rather, he seemed to be positioning himself as a higher, more consequential authority. His actions and rhetoric began affecting more than just his bank account or domestic affairs. The Holy Land came into play.

From 2018-2020, the self-proclaimed strong Christian President set out to achieve Mideast peace between the Israelis and Palestinians. To do so, he commissioned his own son-in-law to broker the deal. His son-in-law was a speculative real estate businessman. To be clear, he had no discernible credentials that screamed "broker of peace in the Middle East." To some, the whole thing was laughable and fishy. In September of 2020, the bombastic billionaire boasted from the balcony of the White House "We're here this afternoon to change the course of history. After decades of division and conflict, we mark the dawn of a new Middle East…will serve as a foundation for a comprehensive peace across the entire region." Of course, the signing of the Abraham Accords was hardly world-altering. This "historic" agreement of peace in the Middle East was not a game-changer. It was only an agreement between Israel, Bahrain, and the United Arab Emirates. Israel has never been at war with either of those nations. Nothing changed. The verse Jeremiah 6:14 immediately hit me: "They dress the wound of my people as though it were not serious. 'Peace, peace' they say, when there is no peace."

As I write this chapter in October of 2023, all hell has broken loose in the Mideast. The Islamic terrorist group Hamas centered in the Gaza Strip of Israel conducted a devastating attack on Jewish Israelis. The Israelis have responded and attacked back with the goal of eradicating Hamas. As this unfolds, countless civilians will likely become victims. It remains to be seen if a full-scale air and ground war will break out in the Holy Land, but there is a very real threat that this conflict will be prolonged. It could spread throughout the region and beyond. It is perhaps the most grave and consequential time in Israel's history since it garnered statehood in 1948.

> Update as of July, 2024 (just before publishing): Israeli forces have maintained their version of a "war on terror" in Gaza. Israel's death count sits around 1,400, mostly

> from the initial terror attack on October 7, 2023. Meanwhile, over 39,000 Palestinian civilians have been killed by Israeli forces. A staggering two million have been displaced and forced out of their homes. A humanitarian crisis has unfolded, and many have labeled it a genocide. The United Nations has called on Israel for an immediate ceasefire. Meanwhile, the Islamic terror group Hezbollah has begun to enter the fray. This book is only focused on this conflict as it potentially relates to Biblical prophecy. Biblical prophecy centers around Israel and Jerusalem, and thus the references in this book will often view the conflict through this lens. Still, it feels imperative to update the status of this conflict and the extent of human suffering in Gaza. The region remains very unstable geopolitically, and it likewise remains highly critical in a prophetic sense.

The prophecies of Revelation and Daniel seem very relevant again. Looking back a few years, those boastful declarations that our subject is the Chosen One and that he has brokered peace in the Holy Land - all that is no longer laughable. To many, it is spine-tingling frightening. You don't have to read on to know where this is going. You are already hearing about this war in the Middle East everyday. You are hearing about it on the news, at the water cooler, in social settings everywhere. You are hearing about it in apocalyptic terms from people you never knew were religious. You are hearing it is a sign of the times. You are hearing of wars and rumors of wars. You have heard him say "Peace, peace" when there is no peace.

Of course, the red-hatted politician is running for President again. And of course, he is as popular with my fellow evangelical Christians as ever. He no doubt has a plan for peace everywhere, including in the Mideast. Some say he will claim he knows more about it than anyone. It is inevitable that he may soon declare after publication of this book that he and he alone can solve this problem and broker peace. He might even say he could do it in one day. Suddenly, his thoughts are not on porn stars and casinos and reality tv hosting. His concerns and words seem more consequential in apocalyptic ways.

As of writing in 2023, the red-hatted politician is currently indicted 91 times in four jurisdictions. He is accused of all sorts of crimes. In New York, he has been charged with 34 felony counts regarding falsifying business records to conceal hush-money payments to porn star Stormy Daniels. In Florida, he faces 40 felony counts of willfully retaining classified documents and a conspiracy to obstruct retrieval of said documents. In Washington DC, he has been charged with four felony counts, including conspiracy to defraud the United States, conspiracy to obstruct an official proceeding (of Congress), obstructing said official proceeding, and conspiracy against civil rights (voter suppression). In Georgia, he faces 13 counts, including racketeering, solicitation of public officials to violate their oath of office, conspiracy to commit forgery, conspiracy to file false documents, and making false statements. He was found liable by a jury in a separate civil suit for sexually molesting a woman in a department store dressing room. He has been found liable in another civil suit for massive business and tax fraud to the tune of $250 million. He was previously found liable for defrauding students in his fake university. Up until now, he refuses to ever meaningfully testify in his own defense, unwilling or unable to definitively clear his name. He rarely defends himself under oath on the witness stand. He only defends himself while not under oath in arenas (social media, rallies, interviews) where the truth is optional. Some say this is the very definition of a "man of lawlessness."

And yet, this man seems to go unscathed among his supporters, many of them evangelical Christians. The more he is indicted, the more many love him. The more the law opposes him, the more many support him. Why do some say he is lawless? His defenses for his crimes have been just that. He has claimed immunity as President, that the law literally does not apply to him. He has claimed that he is not the guilty one; rather, it is the entire judicial system that is guilty and corrupt. He has claimed all of this - the law is corrupt, the Capitol police officers are corrupt, the FBI is corrupt, the judges are corrupt, the jurors are corrupt, the district attorneys and prosecutors are corrupt, his fellow Republicans (who testify against him) are corrupt, and his former lawyer Michael Cohen is corrupt. The man who claimed he could commit murder on Fifth Avenue and not lose any votes has proven he can indeed ignore any and all laws and not lose much support. He is not losing votes from the very people who claim to love law and order and morality and peace. He has convinced them that HE is the law - believe him and him alone. Some would argue this is the man of lawlessness personified.

With each indictment, polls have shown his support increase among white evangelicals. In effect, the more lawless he becomes, the more they support him. Of all the issues raised, this may be the most chilling. Another historical figure was persecuted by the government of his day. His name was Jesus Christ. The optics here are obvious. Many of my fellow evangelical Christians are increasingly treating this man as a deity, as a savior of America and themselves. The more he is held to account for his crimes, the more they view this as a Savior being persecuted by the government. He all but tells them this. He tells them that first the government is coming for him, then it is coming for them all, for them and their churches and their religion. He alone is that sacrifice to save them from the forces of evil, the "deep state." Some believe he is ordained by God (flaws and all) to liberate America. They view America as a special place, as God's chosen land. They believe America is a Christian nation for Christians only, despite it being founded on the premise of separation of Church and State. Many are taking him at his word and treating him as the literal "Chosen One" to restore America as a Christian paradise. But for Christians, we read in Scripture that the earth is temporary, that God has prepared a special place for the faithful in heaven, not on the earth. This truth seems to have been forgotten.

Many of his followers have been described as being in a cult. It is a cult of personality, of his personality. They believe his every word. His words this past year have turned extremely apocalyptic. In March of 2023, he held his first political rally of his new campaign. Of all the cities he could choose, he selected Waco, Texas. The city of Waco, of course, was the site of the April 1993 FBI attack on David Koresh and the Branch Davidians. For the average American outside of Texas, Waco has become synonymous with this event. The Branch Davidians were an apocalyptic religious cult. The FBI raid involved search warrants for illegal weapons violations and alleged sexual assaults. The event is etched in the collective memory of Americans, as the raid turned deadly and the cult's compound was burned to the ground.

While the cult's leaders were militant and fired upon federal agents, some still view the event as an example of the "deep state" suppressing religious freedom. These are the same words being used by the red-hatted politician. The overall religious symbolism is unmistakable. The red-hatted politician is a divine leader ordained by God, a leader not being prosecuted for real crimes, but rather being persecuted for leading his faithful flock to a mythical promised land.

If I sound like I am being hard on my fellow evangelicals, I am. The entire point of fellowship in a church is to exhort one's fellow believers to stay on the path of righteousness, not to stand silent while a ravenous wolf deceives. I am not alone. Scores of current and former evangelical leaders and preachers are not fooled by this man either. They are speaking out in increasingly large numbers. And they are suffering for it. Preachers are being fired or driven out of their churches for speaking against this man. They are getting driven out for preaching from the Word of God rather than a political playbook. Christian authors are speaking out too, only to receive harassment and threats. If you are reading this, rest assured I agonized for months on whether to publish or not. Some of his supporters aren't known for turning the other cheek - they intimidate with threats of violence.

I would be remiss if I did not mention fundraising and how it relates to Christians. This very wealthy man famously boasted he was not a normal politician, he would be self-funding his campaigns and not take donations. He insisted he would not accept a salary or any money as President. Fast-forward to 2023 and I get spam mail and emails and texts daily to give this alleged billionaire money, that he is ordained by God. Millions of evangelicals across the country get the same correspondence.

At the same time, a different message is being spread at rallies and on social media. The message is that immigrants and foreign people and poor people of color are not human. They are not of

God like us. They are vermin, like rats. They poison our blood. Is it any wonder that charitable giving from evangelicals to the less fortunate is reportedly way down? Do you think he is encouraging Christians to donate money to poor people in Africa and elsewhere? Or is Sally Struthers feeding starving black kids now considered woke? It is for the reader to decide. Again, donations to Christian organizations and charities are reportedly way down. Donations to this man from evangelicals are way up. Are Christians funneling their money away from charity and to this man's campaign and legal defense fund instead? Jesus was born in a barnyard stable and lived a meager life free of earthly treasures and possessions. This man still lives in a fortress by the sea. He claimed in court filings it is valued at over $1 billion. Per the Bible, the love of money is the root of all evil.

Above all things, being a true Christian is about forgiveness. Jesus was the sacrifice for all mankind to save them from their own sin. To be a Christian is to ask forgiveness from God, to repent. As a born again believer in Christ, I ask for forgiveness daily. I fall short of the glory of God regularly, and I thank Jesus for his sacrifice and ask for forgiveness of my many sins. This is Christianity. In his own words and multiple times in 2015 and 2016 (easily verified by searchable news clips), the red-hatted politician indicated he has never asked God for forgiveness. The same man who claimed to be tax-audited due to his strong Christianity claimed he doesn't see a reason to ask for forgiveness. He literally said he does good, he doesn't do many bad things. The optics are obvious - he is telegraphing that he is like Jesus, sinless and blameless. The Bible states that only God, only Jesus Christ is without sin or blame. Jesus was the spotless, blameless Lamb of God (John 1:29). Again, Matthew 7:15 warns us about wolves in sheep's clothing. But the question remains, was the Bible really warning us about a Beast in Lamb's clothing?

In the movie Indiana Jones and The Last Crusade, the film climaxes with Indy entering the lair which hides the Holy Grail, the cup of Jesus. The ancient room houses hundreds of chalices, but only one is the true grail. Of course, the Nazi villain selects the most ornate cup, made of solid gold and precious jewels. It is tall and regal, the chalice of an earthly king. It is for the reader to decide if this is the type of cup this man with his red hats and mansion by the sea and gold-plated bathroom fixtures would choose. Does he inspire others to choose this cup and all it symbolizes (earthly riches and power)? These are the very things Jesus warns against in Matthew 6:19-20. Of course, in the film, drinking from this cup brings death, a poor choice. The cup of Jesus is assuredly the most humble, the plainest and least grand of the bunch, the cup of a poor carpenter, the cup of the meek who shall inherit the earth (Matthew 5:5). This true holy grail, this cup of Jesus, is the exact opposite of everything that the red-hatted politician cherishes or espouses. Like Indiana Jones, one should choose wisely.

It is clear from Scripture that some Christians will be fooled by the Antichrist. They will not see him coming for who he really is. It is up to the reader to decide if that is what is happening here.

The Beast will not just be a deceiver; he will also be a dictator. When calamity and tribulations befall the world, he will seize the moment and ascend to worldwide power. As such, it is essential to examine the red-hatted politician in this light. Is he speaking in apocalyptic language? Is he preparing us for a dictatorship? Is he telegraphing a new world order?

Chapter 16: The Beast Reveals Himself

Up until now, this book has tried to frame things in a mostly non-political way. The issues discussed in this book first and foremost concern spiritual and apocalyptic matters, not political activism. At its core, this book is not about economic or foreign policy, social justice reform, abortion rights, or any hot-button culture war issues. It is not about red states or blue states or cable news network preferences. It is not about America as a global force versus American isolationism. However, given the questions raised in previous chapters, there is obviously some overlap. In this chapter, it is necessary to examine the upcoming (at time of publishing) 2024 presidential election, or more precisely what one candidate is saying and telegraphing. If we are indeed steamrolling towards a new world order, are there any new clues staring us in the face? Are we already being told that the apocalypse is at hand?

In most election cycles in the United States, we know the routine. An incumbent president not on his second term will run again for office. The opposition party will have several viable candidates. Those candidates are slowly whittled down to one during the primaries and national conventions. From there, one republican and one democrat square off in the general election. We get bombarded with mail and television ads for each candidate. In modern days, our email inboxes and text messaging apps get flooded with election spam too. We are asked to donate money. We watch political debates. The candidates bicker over economic policy, the national debt, military budgets, foreign affairs, current events, cultural issues, etc. We go to the polls and vote. A winner is declared. The winning candidate is inaugurated into office, without incident.

CHAPTER 16: THE BEAST REVEALS HIMSELF

The year 2024 is vastly different. At the time of writing, we are still in the primary phase. It is unclear if the incumbent (an elderly octogenarian) will be a final nominee. The red-hatted politician is cruising towards nomination, but four criminal trials could derail that. The backdrop for all of this is the Capitol riot on January 6, 2021 and the ensuing aftermath. The country is polarized and divided, not just over issues, but over truth and justice.

One candidate has a devout loyal following that believe his every word. If he says he won, he won. If he says thousands of reporters are fake and fraudulent, then his followers believe they are the fake media. If he says countless judges and prosecutors and FBI officials are all part of an evil "deep state" out to get them, they believe him. If his allies contradict him or are deemed "disloyal", they are fired, primaried, harassed, or called names. They are called RINOs, thugs, incompetent, a disaster, etc. Facts and evidence and critical thinking have become secondary to his words. He telegraphed this cult of personality years ago by proclaiming he could commit murder and not lose any votes. A sizable portion of the population has acquiesced to his message and means.

As a key reminder, the Book of Revelation portrays the Beast as a vindictive authoritarian who will demand absolute loyalty. No man will be able to buy or sell goods without loyalty to the Beast. That loyalty will be required through displaying his trademark, a prerequisite for buying and selling presumably anything - food, water, clothes, medicines, diapers, etc. Scripture also tells us that those who refuse will face the wrath of the Beast, including persecution and death. The acceptance of the "mark of the Beast" is not optional. Life under the Beast during the

Tribulation is portrayed as brutal and intense. There will be wars and fighting and natural disasters and plagues and a whole host of biblical hardships. The only way to survive, seemingly, would be to acquiesce and show loyalty to the Beast and his authoritarian regime. It will be an impossible choice for those alive during that time. Accept the Beast and suffer eternal damnation (Revelation 14:9-10), or reject the mark of the Beast and refuse loyalty and worship toward the Beast and face starvation and persecution, perhaps even decapitation and death (Revelation 20:4).

This book poses one simple question: "Is He?" It is impossible to know. One can only look for clues. So in some ways, I am asking "Could he be?"At this time, as the 2024 Presidential race heats up, I am looking for those clues. And they are not hard to find. They are everywhere around us in the headlines and on videotape and on the candidate's own social media. Yes, I am listening to this candidate and what he is saying, what he is telegraphing should he regain his position as the most powerful man on earth. What would his second term look like? Is he speaking and acting differently than before? Is he using apocalyptic language? Is he preparing his followers for a battle and violence? Specifically, is he causing good God-fearing, Jesus-loving people to become more aggressive, to become more accepting of violence as a means to an end? Is he telling us about authoritarian actions he would take involving the military? Is he changing hearts and minds of millions, molding them into loyal subjects that will not dare question his words and actions? Are his former loyal advisors and confidants trying to warn us? Is he intimidating and threatening those who speak against him? To be clear, is he acting like the Man of Lawlessness? Is he acting like the Beast? Let's unpack it all.

CHAPTER 16: THE BEAST REVEALS HIMSELF

Previously, this book has already detailed how this man fits the moniker of "Beast" metaphorically. He is a titan in most every way. He is extravagantly wealthy. He is infinitely famous and well-known worldwide. He is brash and combative and has a sharp tongue for any who challenge him. He is a self-proclaimed genius and consistently brags that he knows more about most any subject than even the experts. He dodged the draft and never served in the military, and yet he claimed he knew more about military strategy than even the generals. He has led a national movement and ideology in his name, raising hundreds of millions in donations despite telling his followers he was so rich he wouldn't need their donations. His power and clout is undeniable and perhaps unprecedented. He is a figurative beast of personality and influence.

Likewise, this book has already detailed how this man fits the moniker of "Man of Lawlessness." It almost goes without saying. Again, he telegraphed this by claiming he could commit murder and not lose votes. Who else even thinks such a thing, much less says it? He is the most litigious leader in the history of the world. He is constantly embroiled in lawsuits, as both the plaintiff or defendant. He was criminally indicted (91 counts of criminal activity) in four different jurisdictions. He was found liable for fraud in a massive civil suit. He was found civilally liable for sexual assault. He was successfully sued for defrauding students at the University bearing his name. He inspired the first ever widespread domestic assault on our nation's Capitol, or at least that is what those who have been convicted have said - he was their inspiration. He calls prosecutors, judges, law clerks, and members of law enforcement corrupt, radical thugs. He tried to stay in power despite losing an election and despite losing all subsequent legal challenges. He seems to act as if he is above the law, or perhaps that he IS the law.

All of that has been detailed in this book. Now, it seems most crucial to examine what he is saying and thinking currently. What is he planning in the future, in his own words?

In March 2023, the red-hatted politician told an adoring crowd at the Conservative Political Action Conference (CPAC) that "I am your justice…I am your retribution." His message was that his prosecution for his alleged crimes is really an attack on his followers, that they will endure the same persecution (even though they have not committed the same alleged crimes at all). Per his own words, justice and the rule of law are not absolute or codified. He is justice. He is retribution. His message has seemingly resonated; his poll numbers are on the rise. He is their martyr. The Bible instructs us on this subject. "Do not take revenge, my dear friends, but leave room for God's wrath, for it is written 'It is mine to avenge; I will repay'" (Romans 12:19). By claiming that he will be their justice and retribution, it seems he is fulfilling the role and authority that the Bible says is God's and God's alone.

In isolation, these comments of retribution and wrath are one thing. We all have urges for revenge, at least on a small scale in our personal lives. In the context of countless political rallies where millions heap praises upon him while wearing his trademark or name on their foreheads, the words are more chilling. To them, he is more than just another candidate. Takeaway - he wants retribution and revenge, and he is inspiring his supporters to want that too.

The red-hatted politician indeed claims he is being persecuted. All of his indictments and everyone who speaks against him - it is all a witch hunt. It is political persecution, it is election interference. He speaks with great self-authority on what is true and not. He accuses others of doing what he has done; he projects. Now, he is promising his retribution, not just in theory, but with more specifics. In a rally in New Hampshire in November of 2023, he told the adoring crowd "They did it to me, now I can do it to them." Also in November in an interview with Univision, he indicated that the "weaponization" of the Justice Department against him "could certainly happen in reverse." He incoherently mixed up a metaphor claiming "What they've done is they've released the genie out of the box". (Genies are associated with bottles, and Pandora with the box, but I digress). He has suggested that Mark Milley, his former Joint Chief of Staff of the armed forces, should possibly be executed, an act of revenge for Milley speaking out in a "disloyal" way.

His defenders, including many Christians, are saying "an eye for an eye." He himself says "an eye for an eye." In April 2016, in an interview with WHAM 1180 AM radio personality Bob Lonsberry, he was asked about his favorite Bible verse. He had fumbled this question earlier on the campaign trail and refused an answer. This time, in a rambling reply, he mentioned a snippet of the Old Testament, "an eye for an eye" (a reference to verses in both Exodus and Leviticus). This theme of retaliation and revenge and retribution continues today.

To be clear, in the New Testament, Jesus Christ himself addresses this very Bible verse in unambiguous, stark language. In Matthew 5:38-39, Jesus says "You have heard that it is said 'an eye for an eye and a tooth for a tooth.' But I say to you, do not resist the one who is evil. But if anyone slaps you on the right cheek, turn to him the other also." The language and message is clear. To follow Christ, one must not seek vengeance. One must not demand an eye for an eye. One must turn the other cheek. **For any man to claim his favorite Bible verse is "an eye for an eye" goes against the exact words and teachings of Jesus. This is against Christ or anti-Christ in thought and action. Importantly, he is encouraging other Christians to adopt this position as well.**

The editor in chief of Christianity Today, Russell Moore, addresses this exact issue. Moore was a prominent evangelical preacher in the Southern Baptist Convention. In an interview with NPR in August 2023, Moore offers this account: "Well, it was the result of multiple pastors telling me essentially the same story about quoting the Sermon on the Mount parenthetically in their preaching - turn the other cheek - to have someone come up after and to say, 'where did you get those liberal talking points?' And what was alarming to me is that in most of these scenarios, when the pastor would say, 'I'm literally quoting Jesus Christ', the response would not be 'I apologize.' The response would be 'yes, but that doesn't work anymore. That's weak.' **And when we get to the point where the teachings of Jesus himself are seen as subversive to us, then we're in a crisis.**" Of course, the red-hatted politician has riled up his flock that they cannot be weak. To quote him on January 6, 2021 mere minutes before the violent and deadly insurrection at the Capitol, he preached "Because you'll never take back our country with weakness…And we fight. We fight like hell. And if you don't fight like hell, you're not going to have a country anymore." **When prominent evangelical Christian pastors assert that Jesus' words and teachings are being replaced by those of a new leader, we should pay attention.**

CHAPTER 16: THE BEAST REVEALS HIMSELF

As mentioned elsewhere in this book, Adolf Hitler was a brutal leader who in so many ways fits many of the descriptions of the Beast in the book of Revelation. Of course Hitler is dead and the world continues on, so he is not the great Beast who reigns just before the return of Jesus. But wow, looking back, he checked off so many boxes. He was an authoritarian leader who set a radical fascist agenda. Absolute loyalty and adoration toward him was demanded, complete with a required visual and verbal salute even outside of his presence. He had a clear, distinct mark emblematic of both him and his ideology. The Nazi swastika seems like a cousin of the mark of the Beast (666) prophesied in Revelation. Hitler's attempt to exterminate all the Jews from his country and eventually the earth jives with the religious implications during the Great Tribulation which will involve the Jewish temple and people. With the limited clues the Bible provides about who is the Beast, Adolf Hitler could be the closest blueprint the world has ever seen.

It is in this context that we return to what is happening on the campaign trail in America, the land of the free and global champion of democracy. As unfathomable as it is, one candidate is successfully invoking the words of Adolf Hitler at his political rallies. He is pulling many themes and ideas direct from Hitler's manifesto, "Mein Kampf", and in some cases using the exact same hate speech that Hitler used to rile up his base. It is the same hate speech that Hitler used to dehumanize those of Jewish descent, the same vitriol that enabled the Holocaust. Before millions of Jews were murdered in gas chambers, Hitler convinced enough Germans that the Jews were the enemy within Germany, that they were inferior to Aryans, that they were a dangerous threat that must be squashed. He convinced enough Germans that extreme violent action was justified to eliminate the threat. He used this extreme political rhetoric to amass supreme authority. He carried out that rhetoric in horrific ways that shocked many of his supporters. Many didn't take him at his literal word or appreciate the grave threat he posed until it was too late.

One should not take comparisons to Adolf Hitler lightly or make accusations lightly either. So it is best to let the words speak for themselves and the reader be the judge. The "Mein Kampf" surmised that the greatest threat to Germany was the enemy within. "For never in our history have we been conquered by the strength of our outside enemies but only through our own failings and the enemy in our own camp…The strength of a nation lies, first of all, not in its arms but in its will, and that before conquering the external enemy the enemy at home would have to be eliminated." Hitler transformed this language into murdering millions of Jews.

In a speech on Veteran's Day 2023, the red-hatted politician, speaking in New Hampshire, expressed identical sentiments: "The threat from outside forces is far less sinister, dangerous and grave than the threat from within. Our threat is from within…Despite the hatred and anger of the radical left lunatics who want to destroy our country, we will make America great again." To be clear, his base is being primed and poked and prodded with this persuasive language. The suggestion is that 'radical left lunatics' (a term he has applied to liberals and democrats) are more dangerous than the threat posed even by foreign terrorists or dictators. Most readers know what America has done with terrorists at Guantanamo Bay. Is it being suggested that his political enemies or even all liberals deserve a similar or harsher fate?

CHAPTER 16: THE BEAST REVEALS HIMSELF

Hitler and the "Mein Kampf" warned about German blood being poisoned by outsiders, especially the Jews. "And so this poison was allowed to enter the national bloodstream and infect public life without the government taking any effectual measures to master the course of the disease…for an institution practically surrenders its existence when it is no longer determined to defend itself with all the weapons at its command…All the great civilizations of the past became decadent because the original creative race died out, as a result of contamination of the blood." We know how Hitler attempted to purify his country's 'blood' and what 'weapons' he used to actualize this hateful rhetoric.

In an interview with The National Pulse on October 5th, 2023, the red-hatted politician also spoke about the blood of America being polluted by immigrants and threatening the 'real' America. "Nobody has any idea where these people are coming from, and we know they come from prisons. We know they come from mental institutions and insane asylums. We know they're terrorists. Nobody has ever seen anything like we're witnessing right now. It is a very sad thing for our country. It's poisoning the blood of our country." His comments and rhetoric over the years have shown these words do not necessarily apply just to illegal, undocumented immigrants. He has supported white supremacists ("fine people"), called for bans on all Muslim immigrants, and favored immigration of peoples of northern European descent.

Robert P. Jones with Religion News Service penned a fascinating article in November 2023 regarding these issues and the shift in rhetoric spewing forth from the red-hatted politician. Entitled "With 'vermin', ***** crosses fully into Nazi territory", the article gets right to the point. Search for and read this article. As Jones points out, Hitler's manifesto the "Mein Kampf" uses the word "vermin" three times and "rats" four. The Jews were referred to in these terms and as pests. "The time seemed to have arrived for proceeding against the whole Jewish gang of public pests...While the flower of the nation's manhood was dying at the front, there was time enough at home at least to exterminate this vermin." Hitler did indeed exterminate the perceived vermin in concentration camps and gas chambers.

At the same Veteran's Day speech in New Hampshire referenced above, would you believe that the red-hatted politician used the word "vermin" too? What are the odds? Is this a common word? "We pledge to you we will root out the communists, Marxists, fascists and radical left thugs that live like vermin within the confines of OUR country that lie and steal and cheat on elections. They'll do anything, whether legally or illegally, to destroy America and to destroy the American dream." Again, this language serves to dehumanize fellow Americans and cast those who disagree politically as an enemy that must be exterminated or eradicated. To drive this point home, the red-hatted politician's own campaign spokesman, Steven Cheung, confirmed this sentiment. The Washington Post had requested comments from the campaign, pointing out that the language of the candidate seemed to invoke Hitler and the "Mein Kampf." Cheung replied "Those who try to make that assertion are clearly snowflakes...and their entire existence will be crushed when President ***** returns to the White House." Their entire existence will be crushed.

Of course, hyperbole is one thing. Is the candidate simply being dramatic and speaking figuratively? Or does he have plans to use the military to literally weed out the "vermin"?

There has been an onslaught of media reports about the

authoritarian nature of the red-hatted politician's campaign. It isn't just the generic language that echoes Hitler. Rather, the candidate is giving specifics of what he would do if he returns to power. Additionally, journalists are reporting on the plans his former staffers and confidants have drawn up, entitled "Project 2025." They are openly discussing these plans on podcasts. Again, this book is not a book about forms of government (democracy versus republic versus socialism versus communism versus fascism, etc). However, as it concerns the book of Revelation's treatment of the Beast, language and rhetoric and plans of an authoritarian nature are very much relevant to this book. The Beast will be an authoritarian who demands absolute loyalty. If an American Presidential candidate (leading the polls) is signaling he too will be an authoritarian that demands absolute loyalty, we should pay attention. What is the red-hatted politician planning, and why does it matter?

Inexplicably, the red-hatted politician is telling us directly that he aspires to truly be a man of lawlessness. It is unbelievable. On the campaign trail and in televised town hall campaign events, he has indicated he would rule as "a dictator on day one." Dictators rule as lawless or above the law. Of course, some see him simply mocking news reports of his shift towards authoritarianism. He wouldn't really be a lawless dictator, right?

In his numerous legal battles to attempt to stay out of prison, his lawyers are also arguing that he is above the law. They are arguing that as President, he has full immunity to do any crime imaginable (even murder) and the criminal justice system cannot prosecute. He has argued this very point on his social media accounts and at political rallies. It seems he believes this "Presidential immunity" only applies to him, as he still plans to prosecute President Biden (who would somehow not have the same "Presidential immunity"). He is undeniably arguing that he is the law. He is above the law, and he can single-handedly decide who has violated the law. Does this sound like a man of lawlessness?

He is attacking the judicial system like never before. Those who attempt to prosecute him are coined as "deranged thugs." Judges who rule against him are "corrupt." Witnesses and jurors are equally vilified. His supporters who commit crimes and are convicted felons are labeled as innocent "hostages." He is redefining the law on his own terms with himself at the center, above the law. Is this a man of lawlessness?

The reports of his shift towards authoritarianism really snowballed in late 2023. Most every major media outlet and newspaper took notice. In his stump speeches and rallies and social media posts, the red-hatted politician started insinuating that he would prosecute his political opponents, including former foes like the Obamas and Clintons, as well as President Biden and his administration and Cabinet. He likewise indicated he would go after former allies who "betrayed" him. He suggested former Joint Chief Chairman Mark Milley should be executed. He did not refute or disagree with those supporters suggesting Mike Pence (his own Vice President) should be hanged. He has suggested prosecution of Bill Barr, his own Attorney General. He telegraphed that to resist absolute loyalty to him was to risk one's life, both figuratively (potential jail time) and literally (potential execution). Again, his lawyers even argued on his behalf that as president, he could assassinate political rivals legally (if 34 loyal Senators agreed not to impeach him for it.) He adopted these legal arguments for his campaign speeches. Notably, he implies these people should be punished without a trial. He has already determined their guilt and punishment, absent of due process. Going after one's political opponents in this manner is the act of a dictator. This is what Vladimir Putin and Kim Jong Un do. This does not happen in America, yet.

In other speeches and social media posts, the red-hatted politician suggested severe retribution against any media outlets that were not loyal. Specifically, he raised the prospect of shutting down MSNBC should he become President again. Of course, in America, we enjoy freedom of the press. To ban any media on a political basis is the act of a dictator. This is what Vladimir Putin and Kim Jong Un do. This does not happen in America, yet.

Also in these campaign speeches and social media posts, the red-hatted politician suggested he would defund or eliminate government bedrocks like the Department of Justice, the IRS, and the Department of Homeland Security. These agencies dictate the rule of law and order, keep our nation secure from threats from abroad and within, and keep our nation financially solvent through collection of taxes. Not coincidentally, all three agencies have tried to hold the red-hatted politician accountable either legally or financially. It seems they are being targeted for not being loyal to him and him alone. This does not happen in America, yet. America is not a monarchy or a dictatorship, yet.

As indicated in news reports and podcasts by loyalists, a series of extreme measures are planned should the red-hatted politician win this election. A group of loyalists and advisors have formed a think-tank linked to the Heritage Foundation and are allegedly working on "Project 2025." If true, this sounds like a "new world order" on a national level, if not global. The architects are working on legal justifications for a host of executive orders and actions. Job applicants for the new regime are being graded not on skill or experience, but rather on pure loyalty to the leader. Most shockingly, Project 2025 includes plans for the Insurrection Act to be declared in America. In effect, U.S. troops would be deployed to the streets to maintain "law and order" against anyone who dissents or protests against the red-hatted politician. This does not happen in America, yet. America is not a monarchy, a dictatorship, or a military state with an authoritarian who demands absolute loyalty, yet. America is not Revelation chapter 13, yet.

Steven Levitsky, a Harvard government professor, perhaps summed up best why this is alarming. Speaking to the Guardian: "This is one of the most openly authoritarian campaigns I've ever seen. You have to go back to the far-right authoritarians in the 1930's in Europe or in 1970's Latin America to find the kind of dehumanizing and violent language that (the red-hatted politician) is starting to consistently use."

Of all the rhetoric coming out of this campaign, it is the use of apocalyptic language from the candidate himself that may be the most shocking. Again, the campaign kicked off with a speech in Waco, Texas with the red-hatted politician declaring "I am your retribution." Increasingly and consistently, apocalyptic language is being used to describe America and to describe his crusade for power. America "is going to hell", his political opponents "can go to hell", this election is "the Final Battle" (Revelation 19), the court cases against him have "opened up that seal" (Revelation 8:1). Time and time again, the self-anointed "chosen one" has used biblical language to paint himself and his movement in Messianic, return-of-Jesus ways.

To see the effect his MAGA movement is having on

evangelicals, one need only walk into certain evangelical churches on Sunday morning. If you don't hear about the Maga fight as good versus evil from the preacher, you might hear about it from a parishioner. Just ask. If online videos are more your style, a simple youtube search can generate numerous interviews with supporters who claim the red-hatted politician is either the Messiah or Messianic or sent from God.

Capitalizing on this fervor, the campaign itself double-downed on the red-hatted politician's anointed status. In a video entitled "God made *****", we hear "And on June 14, 1946, God looked down on his planned paradise and said 'I need a caretaker,' so God gave us *****...'I need somebody who can shape an ax but wield a sword, who had the courage to step foot in North Korea, who can make money from the tar of the sand, who can turn liquid to gold…' so God made *****. God had to have somebody willing to go into the den of vipers, to call out the fake news for their tongues as sharp as serpents, the poison of vipers is on their lips…so God made *****. God said 'I need somebody who will be strong and courageous, who will not be afraid or terrified of the wolves when they attack, a man who cares for the flock, a shepherd to mankind who will never leave or forsake them…' so God made *****.

For the unchurched, I'll add context. In the gospels of the New Testament, we read that God sent Jesus to earth. Jesus did similar things as listed above, including turning water into wine, going into the figurative den of vipers and upsetting the establishment, calling out fake prophets. Jesus was the "Good Shepherd", caring for and saving the sinful flock that is mankind. To be clear, this campaign video is beyond blasphemous. It is beyond sacrilegious. It is chillingly eerie to the prophecies of Revelation indicating the

Beast will be worshiped.

Yes, he is actively campaigning as a Messiah figure, as a gift sent from God to establish America as God's paradise. Upon seeing the campaign video, many pastors and clergy members spoke out. In their January 8, 2024 article "Iowan Pastors denounce 'God Made *****' video", Yahoo News spoke with Michael Demastus, pastor of the Fort Des Moines Church of Christ. He did not mince his words, saying "I find it absolutely sickening, period. (The red-hatted politician) is not the Messiah… Many other evangelical pastors find that video offensive."

> Update at final edit: In June of 2024, the red-hatted politician held a rally in Las Vegas, Nevada. His opening speakers and allies left little doubt about whether or not he is campaigning as a Messiah. First, Marjorie Taylor Greene compared him to Jesus Christ, saying they are both convicted felons. The crowd erupted. (She left out that Jesus did not illegally pay off a porn star to stay quiet about sexual sin). More shockingly, the Chair of the Nevada Republican Party, Michael McDonald, said the quiet part out loud. It can't be taken back, it is on video for all to watch on Youtube. "We are here, in Sunset Park, to **worship** and bring back the greatest President we've ever known in our generation."

As far as motive goes, some have suggested several reasons as to why the red-hatted politician could want to become a dictator. First and foremost, he is facing serious legal jeopardy that could result in decades in prison (a de facto life sentence for a senior citizen). Becoming an all-powerful dictator who reshapes codified law could shield him from criminal accountability. He could evade prosecution and deliver on his promised "retribution" against his adversaries.

A second motive to consider may concern his children. Increasingly, many of his well-known adult children are becoming more ingrained in the American political scene. It does not take much imagination to see how a dictator would aspire to pass the leadership baton to his offspring in the future and create a dynasty. His daughter-in-law has already been installed as the co-chair of the RNC.

A third motive to consider involves money. Currently, an American President is required to divest himself of any business interests that could compromise his oath of office. In other words, a President cannot legally profit from being President (other than his salary). The red-hatted politician already blurred the lines on this law once, hosting foreign dignitaries at his Washington D.C. hotel as just one example. It is not hard to see how a dictator could freely use his position of power to profit. A dictator's policies and decisions could theoretically be for sale. As just one example, a dictator could make deals with foreign leaders in exchange for having skyscrapers (bearing his name) erected in foreign cities.

When taken altogether, the evidence is extensive. The red-hatted politician and millions of his supporters are framing his life and his quest for power in biblical terms. His campaign and language has taken on an apocalyptic tone. There is considerable evidence that he may aspire to rule as a dictator on day one. It is up to the reader to decide what it all means. Does this fit the traits that will be seen in the Beast of Revelation? Could the bombastic billionaire aspire to eventually rule as a global dictator? Would he demand absolute loyalty to the point of worship? Does he have the potential motives to do so?

Section 5 -

If it Happens

This book is not an allegation. It is simply considering a hypothetical question, whether the most famous man on earth could actually be the Beast of Revelation. You may have heard Christians say that God uses flawed men to fulfill his will. Is that the case here, only in a different way? Is a wealthy businessman and politician the unwitting Beast in prophecy? Is He?

In the previous chapters, you have been given a crash course in evangelical end times prophecy. A case has been made for why we could be living at the end of human history on earth. Moreover, you have learned about the Antichrist, the prophesied Beast of Revelation that will come to rule the entire world. There has been thoughtful discourse about what the Beast will be like in terms of persona and demeanor. You have read how countless evangelical Christians have come to champion a bombastic leader who has presented himself as a Messianic figure. You have learned about the mark of the Beast. You have seen that the mark may already be out there. You have seen that this man's trademark may be the actual mark as described in Revelation.

This last section is the toughest section to write for this author. It is not enough that I may see the signs in front of me. It is not enough that something could be true. To have any real credibility, I must present a very hypothetical but plausible version of how events could play out. No matter how far-fetched, it has to be possible. To be frank, the events as depicted in the Book of Revelation (where one man rules over the entire world) seem very impossible. The challenge, therefore, is to imagine a realistic, believable scenario in which we transition from the status quo of today into a world that matches up with the apostle John's cataclysmic visions in Revelation.

This book has already posed a hypothetical question to the reader - is the red-hatted politician the Beast in waiting? The question now shifts to how. How could he rule the entire world? How could he become the Beast? Who helps him?

Up to this point, I have mentioned the "second beast" or "false prophet" of Revelation mostly in passing. This has been intentional. In this last section, though, it is crucial to discuss this second beast. As mentioned in Section 2 earlier, passages from Revelation give many descriptors about this man and the qualities and powers he possesses. This book is first and foremost about one man, the Man of Lawlessness, the first Beast, the Antichrist. But it seems he will have an enabler, a right-hand man that helps him assume full worldwide domination.

For the first time in any published book, you will read new extremely detailed, compelling evidence, corroborated by Scripture, on who this second beast could possibly be. For the first time in recorded human history, one man may truly fit the Biblical descriptions. You will be given compelling evidence on not just the who, but also the why and how - what motives and capabilities could lead him to unknowingly be a key piece of biblical prophecy. This is not an allegation or indictment, just a hypothetical reading and analysis of Scripture.

If the end times are indeed close at hand and the Beast is alive on earth, where do we go from here? How could a man who only has potential power (election pending) over one nation transform himself into a true worldwide leader? It seems impossible. How could that man use his trademark and name and power and connections to usher in a new worldwide financial system with himself at the head? It seems preposterous. And yet, the Book of Revelation clearly depicts a new world order during the Tribulation, those last years just before Jesus himself returns.

Many evangelical Christians in America believe one key event will happen just at the start of the Tribulation. Perhaps that one event will cause the Tribulation to begin and change our technological, electronic modern world in every way. This momentous happening could change everything in the blink of an eye. If you've come this far, perhaps you'd like to journey a little farther down this rabbit hole of Revelation that just maybe isn't so far-fetched at all. It's time to revisit the Rapture.

Chapter 17: The Rapture Envisioned

Earlier in this book, the Rapture was discussed. Again, this is the vanishing of devout Christians from the earth in the blink of an eye. It conjures up an image of chaos, confusion and carnage. It is the last event to take place on earth before the prophesied Tribulation. In chapter 3 of Revelation, we read that the faithful will be spared from the coming trials and tribulations set to fall upon the earth's inhabitants.

Chapters 4-7 of the Book of Revelation take a dramatic turn. The apostle John is transported to heaven and writes of all he sees and hears. Per Revelation 4:1-2, he is "in the spirit", "whisked into heaven", and shown "the things which must be hereafter." Revelation is full of symbolism, but this seems like a clear turning point, a line in the sand. The Church age is over. His immediate snatching away into heaven could represent the Rapture of believers away from the earth as the great Tribulation begins. He doesn't see the Rapture here, but he possibly experiences it. Others believe he witnesses the Rapture in Revelation 7:9 - "After this I looked, and there before me (in heaven) was a great multitude that no one could count, from every nation, tribe, people and language, standing before the Throne and before the Lamb." After this and for the remainder of Revelation, John goes on to describe the Great Tribulation, The Beast, the false prophet, the mark of the Beast, the final battle of Armageddon and the return of Jesus to the earth.

A curious event occurs in Revelation 6:12-13. A "sixth seal" is opened and calamity befalls the earth. There is a great earthquake (one of many mentioned in Revelation), the sun goes black, and the moon "became as blood." In verse 13, "And the stars of heaven fell onto the earth." This is the last seal opened before John sees the "great multitude" in heaven. As referenced above, it is unclear if this event occurs early during the Tribulation just after the Rapture or beforehand. It is possible that it is describing the calamity on earth just before the Rapture comes to pass, the Church age ends, and the great Tribulation begins.

The stars falling to earth are especially curious. We know that literal stars (hot and big like our sun, itself a star) cannot literally fall onto the earth without completely destroying our planet and all life forms. The "stars" of Revelation 6:13 are more likely just what John saw as stars, perhaps meteorites striking the earth. The falling stars could also be modern weapons of war, as missiles and rockets fired at night resemble "stars" falling from the heavens. Or perhaps he saw something else, something exactly resembling stars, something newer and unique to our modern world, something that did not even exist back in 1948 when Israel was reborn into statehood. More to come on this…

> As has happened often while writing this book over the past two years, world events and headlines get my attention and cause me to edit my writing. This section is an edit and has been added in. I am writing it on October 14, 2023. The headlines of October 2023 have slapped me in the face. The following is perhaps a coincidence, or maybe it is a warning that we are quickly nearing the end of days. To be clear, no man knows the day or hour of Christ's return or of the Rapture. Nobody.
>
> To recap, Revelation 6:12-13 reads: "And I beheld when he opened the sixth seal, and lo, there was a great earthquake, and the sun became black as sackcloth, and the moon became as blood, And the stars of heaven fell

unto the earth, even as a fig tree casteth her untimely figs, when she is shaken of a mighty wind".

On October 7, 2023, a powerful earthquake struck the Middle East in Afghanistan. Thousands perished. This alone did not strike me as prophetic, as we hear of earthquakes around the world often.

On October 14, 2023, there was a rare annular "ring of fire" eclipse of the sun visible here from earth. It was broadcast worldwide on tv and the internet for all to see. The sun went fully dark save a tiny ring of light, the "ring of fire." In two weeks on October 28, 2023, there is a lunar eclipse of the "blood moon", so named because the moon is expected to give off a reddish hue.

Also, on October 7, 2023, the same day as the horrific earthquake in Afghanistan, the terror cell Hamas attacked Israel, killing just over a thousand. Israel has since retaliated, killing thousands, and a major conflict in the Middle East has broken out, a war in the Holy Land. As I watched the news today, I saw Israeli rockets raining down on the Gaza Strip. At night, these rockets looked like stars falling to earth. I could see how the apostle John would potentially describe it this way, having never seen modern war weapons in the 1st century AD. The use of the fig tree in this verse is what really caught my attention. As mentioned previously, the Bible repeatedly uses the fig tree as a parable for Israel and the Jewish people. The fact that the falling stars are immediately compared to untimely falling figs shook me to my core as I watched Israeli rockets falling from the heavens to the earth.

Second edit: In April of 2024, just before publishing, it feels necessary to add in another edit along the same lines. On April 5, 2024, New York City and the Northeast United States were struck by a rare East Coast earthquake, centered in New Jersey. It was a mild earthquake in force (4.8 on the Richter scale) but shocking due to the highly unusual and densely populated location. It made worldwide headlines. This time I took note.

I knew the total solar eclipse, visible in the United States, was occurring soon on April 8, 2024. Once again, a newsworthy earthquake and a solar eclipse occurred the same week. I remembered there had been a lunar eclipse a couple weeks earlier in March, though there was no mention of it being a "blood moon" or red in color. Still, I worried that something was about to go down in the Middle East. I felt like a conspiracy theorist convert.

Sure enough, on the night of April 13, 2024, it happened. Cable news networks again cut to scenes of "stars" falling to the earth, this time in Israel. This was the night that Iran, in conjunction with Hezbollah and other Arab factions, conducted airstrikes on Israeli targets. Panic again set in around the globe that a broader regional conflict was breaking out, but tensions cooled a couple days later. Israel did not retaliate as forcefully as feared and instead just maintained their assault on Gaza.

It could all be a coincidence indeed, but the events in October 2023 and April 2024 gave me the chills. It was as if I was seeing the events of the sixth seal of revelation 6:12-13 play out on my tv screen and smartphone in real time, not once but twice. This was the final impetus I needed to actually publish this controversial book, to hell with the consequences. Again, if one interprets the multitude in heaven in Revelation 7 to be the Rapture, then the opening of the sixth seal in Revelation 6 is the LAST event John witnesses on earth before the Rapture. In Revelation 8, the seventh seal is open. Revelation 8:1 chillingly reads "And when he had opened the seventh

> seal, there was silence in heaven about the space of half an hour." This sounds like the beginning of the Tribulation.

Thinking intuitively, imagine the Rapture happens. If overnight and suddenly, every Christian churchgoer vanishes into thin air, it could and should be quite obvious to anyone remaining what has happened. I know if every Buddhist on earth vanished at the same time, I'd be reading and researching Buddhism non-stop to find out what happend, whether it was prophesied, etc. It is the age of information (and dis-information) and we do not live in a vacuum. Non-believers have been exposed to Christian prophecies enough in pop culture at large to figure it out. In much the same way that the Antichrist won't just show up with 666 tattooed on his forehead, one could imagine the Rapture will not ultimately be so straight-forward or obvious.

The last mention of the Church in the book of Revelation before the Tribulation is in chapter 3, and it is a stern warning. Revelation 3:14-22 seems blatantly directed to the Church/Christians alive just before the Antichrist assumes full power. The verses paint a picture of believers who are lukewarm towards the Lord. It paints a picture of believers who have earthly comfort and riches and profess their faith indifferently and inconsistently. It follows that these are the people who will be left behind at the Rapture (along with all non-believers), the Christians who are sidetracked by earthly status and riches and comfort. In the year 2023, this is how a lot of non-believers view Christians of today. Some (not all) seem less concerned with charity and turning the other cheek and loving their enemy and clinging to the teachings of Jesus and spreading the Word of the Lord so that the Holy Spirit can work in individual lives; rather, many seem preoccupied with politics and legislating their faith and passionately supporting what some consider a morally bankrupt 'vessel of God.' They do not realize the hundreds of millions they have turned away from being receptive to Christianity by their own actions and hypocrisy.

The more I contemplate the Rapture, it does make the most sense that the Rapture itself will be the momentous event that allows the Man of Lawlessness to eventually assume full authority over the earth during the Tribulation. It makes the most sense to me that the Rapture be disguised so that it can eventually be explained away by an authoritarian figure in power. The Rapture, and the simultaneous vanishing of presumably millions of people, must be the singular event that leads to the earth changing from hundreds of ruling leaders/governments around the globe to one worldwide leader/authoritarian, namely the great Beast or Antichrist. How could this happen? What scenarios could play out and explanations offered? Where did all the missing people go? I have heard various theories over the years, but none quite added up all the way.

In the 1990s, I remember hearing the Antichrist could be an alien who takes over the earth. Perhaps if several spaceships are recorded over the earth at once (or are photo-shopped as proof), alien abduction would be the excuse for the Rapture. A leader with a plan to fight the "aliens" could emerge in the chaos. Another possibility? Given the current political environment, one could imagine conspiracy theories propagating that militaries around the globe coordinated a simultaneous attack rounding up scores of devout Christians in an act of persecution. History has seen religious persecution, kidnapping, and murder before (the Holocaust), albeit not in one day or worldwide. Still, we could easily imagine that headline scrolling on the banner at the bottom of a cable news channel while the dust settles. A third possibility?

With millions of people missing, the UN could convene and hash out a plan to assert law and order over a suddenly chaotic world. Perhaps one leader could emerge. Other theories are that the world could be in a nuclear war, and amidst the carnage and chaos of a nuclear winter, the Rapture could whisk away millions of believers. Perhaps a leader emerges after the nuclear dust settles.

All of these are possibilities for how the Rapture will be explained away/go unnoticed and the Tribulation begins. I have heard them and more all before - asteroid strike, nuclear war, aliens. But there is a problem. None of these fully explain how or why the world would have just one global leader. They do not fully explain how our world of hundreds of languages and cultures and governments would willingly agree to follow one world leader. They do not fully explain how or why a single, worldwide, mandatory monetary system would come to fruition. They do not fully explain the two beasts of Revelation 13 - one the leader/Antichrist and the other the practical enabler who performs great signs. They do not necessarily explain the "falling stars" of Revelation 6.

There is another theory on how it all unfolds, and it explains it all. Buckle up.

Chapter 18 - The Internet Apocalypse

It was the summer of 1994 - the days were warm, the nights breezy, and all was calm. And then, in the blink of an eye, everything changed. Countless Americans remember where they were on the fateful night of June 17, 1994. They remember where they were when their tv screens showed a most curious site. They remember where they were when they saw a score of police cars slowly pursuing a lone, white Ford Bronco down a bizarrely empty California freeway. Everyone old enough remembers the beginnings of the trial of the century and the case against O.J. Simpson. They remember the chase, the surrender, the murder charges, the prosecutors, the defense attorneys, Judge Ito, Cato Calin, the glove, the acquittal, the grieving families of the victims. Most remember O.J. promising to hunt down the "real killers" for the rest of his life. Yes, the sensational scandal of a celebrity murder trial captured the attention of a nation. Over a decade later in 2006, interest swelled again when O.J. co-authored a book entitled "If I did it: Confessions of the Killer." He didn't confess to the crime per se, but rather he just "hypothesized" how the crime could have been committed. He took the timeline and evidence and imagined how it all happened.

It is in that spirit of hypothesizing that this chapter will address the Rapture, the Tribulation, and the rise of the Beast and false prophet. Think of this chapter as "If it happens, here's how it could happen". Nobody really knows how it will go down. The best anyone can do is apply equal parts Scripture and common sense. The fact is the Bible gives us many clues as to the end of days, and the Bible gives us specific descriptions of events and conditions during the great Tribulation. But, the Bible gives us few clues as to how this drastic change will occur, the change away from our current everyday ho-hum routines and into the post-Rapture world. Envisioning a world with one powerful leader and one mandatory monetary system is a stretch. It takes imagination to conceive of a singular global world order under complete control of one man, the Beast. It is hard to fathom how we go from our modern world with hundreds of sovereign nations - each with their own leaders and governments - to one single ruler for all mankind.

As such, this chapter is just a theory - a well-thought-out theory. It is intended to cause the reader to stop and think, to reflect on how fragile our current way of life is, and to contemplate who could be ready and willing to seize control when the unthinkable happens and why they would do it. That part is key, why they would want to do it - their unique and very public ambitions and personalities and wealth and interest in shaping a new world order. For too long, preachers and prognosticators have assumed that the great Beast of Revelation will just think like Satan and have the Devil's agenda. That imagery is wrong. The Man of Lawlessness is not the devil incarnate. He is a human with human motives. He could be a very flawed man driven by the human impulses that define the worst of us - insatiable greed and ego and the willingness to do anything to satisfy those cravings. If it does come to pass, here's how it could very believably happen.

To imagine the biblical apocalypse in today's world, it is crucial to focus on our technology - both its amazing capabilities and our unprecedented reliance on it. These amazing capabilities (worldwide communication and worldwide financial transactions at the speed of light) are exactly how prophecy can finally be fulfilled on a global scale. Our unprecedented reliance on these technologies could be our downfall, exactly how one or two men easily come to rule the whole world.

Here in America in the year 2023, life for the masses is more advanced than ever, and the prophecies of Daniel 12:4 come to mind. Of course there is economic inequality, inflation, crime, and hundreds of other national and global issues of concern. But in general, for more people than ever, life has never been so advanced and modern. The Lord has blessed many of us. People worldwide have benefited from decades of exponential advances in medicine and technology. We live longer and healthier than generations before us, and we generally have a higher standard of living than generations before us. Think of life a hundred years ago in 1923. Could they even imagine things like the internet, smartphones, giant screen TVs, Alexa, DoorDash, Amazon, sophisticated hospitals, and any other host of modern luxuries and conveniences? For perspective, my grandfather was born in a small wooden house with no electricity or indoor plumbing. Kings of the Middle Ages could only dream of the comfort and excess that the average middle class American enjoys every day. We have air conditioning, furnaces, refrigerators, machines that wash and dry our clothes, airplanes, luxury cruise ships, affordable access to any type of global cuisine we want on demand. We have comfortable shoes and painkillers and cold medicines and antibiotics and the list goes on and on. Some of us spend a substantial amount of our time enjoying leisure activities and pursuing hobbies. This isn't to sugarcoat or ignore the problems we face in our world or our individual lives. Rather, it is a stark reminder of just how far civilization and mankind have come over the centuries, of the technological breakthroughs that permeate our everyday lives. If you can't tell, my favorite ride at Disney World as a kid was the 'Carousel of Progress.'

CHAPTER 18 - THE INTERNET APOCALYPSE

It is these very technological breakthroughs that make the end of the world as described in the Bible finally possible. Consider one example concerning the Beast. Centuries ago, it would have been logistically impossible for the world to have one central ruler. How would people several time zones away on different continents even have heard of this one man, much less be ruled by him in real time. What about people on remote tropical islands? According to Scripture, the Great Tribulation and reign of the Beast is only 3.5 years long. In medieval times, it would have taken more time than that for any powerful emperor or king's armies just to reach and conquer all the ends of the earth, much less establish a new world order. But in modern times, with modern technology and communication, with the advent of advanced internet connectivity worldwide, things are different. We now have the infrastructure and audiovisual capabilities for the Man of Lawlessness to reign supreme. A one-world leader could now theoretically go live (perhaps a slight delay) to all the ends of the earth and communicate with his subjects or generals or whoever. We even have software and artificial intelligence that can translate a person's words into most any language in real time. If the new world order during the Tribulation is indeed something of a military state, we have ships and jets that can move troops and armies in hours and days, not years. We live in a very unique time indeed.

Another key portion of biblical prophecy also seems able to now be fulfilled due to technology. The first section of this book touched on this very issue, but it bears repeating. In Matthew 24:14 and Mark 13:10, it is declared that the gospel (of Jesus) will be proclaimed or preached throughout the whole world as a testimony to all nations, and then the end will come. To be sure, you would have to have lived under a rock in many parts of

America to have never heard of Jesus or that Jesus saves or any version of the tenets of Christianity. And yes, over the last century especially, there have been foreign missionaries and others who have spread Christianity around the globe. This isn't to say Christianity has overtaken the world (many reject it); rather, it seems like a crucial step to fulfilling prophecy, that the gospel reaches all ends of the earth before the end can come.

But still, there are surely peoples and regions of the earth who have never had access to reading a Bible or audibly hearing the testimony of Jesus as the redeemer or savior. That hurdle seems closer than ever to being cleared through technology. At the time of writing, communication satellites are constantly being launched into a low-earth orbit from the east coast of Florida and from southern California. You may have heard of these satellites, and more likely you have surely heard of the CEO launching them.

This well-known entrepreneur and visionary is also the richest man in the world, literally. He really became a household name around the same time that the red-hatted businessman entered politics. In addition to being rich, he has a lot of thoughts and plans and visions for shaping a new, better world. Some of his ideas involve practical technology and innovation, such as self-driving cars. Other ideas and passions seem more, ahem, grand and survival-of-our-species oriented, such as increasing the birth rate/population and colonizing other planets. He is indeed an ambitious visionary who is already re-shaping the future of life on earth.

Among his many forward-looking ventures, Starlink is one of the most interesting. The aim of Starlink, which is a division of SpaceX, is to bring high speed internet access (via satellite) to every inch of the globe. Sure, many of us have internet access seamlessly in our daily lives, enabled via underground cables. But for some areas of the globe, this is not the case. Many areas are too rural or isolated geographically for current internet access. Other people live in countries that lack the infrastructure, or their access to websites is restricted or blocked by governments. As pertains to prophecy, this lack of access could be the final roadblock to all people everywhere hearing the gospel of Jesus Christ.

Worldwide internet access, however, potentially enables the preaching of the Word of the Lord to every person in every language. It is easy to see how that roadblock would be removed should internet access flow freely to every human on earth, and satellites are making that possible. Revelation 14:6-7 further comments on this element of prophecy, in this case during the great Tribulation. "Then I saw another angel flying directly overhead, with an eternal gospel to proclaim to those who dwell on earth, to every nation and tribe and language and people. And he said with a loud voice 'Fear God and give him glory, for the hour of his judgment has come, and worship him who made heaven and earth, the sea and the springs of water.'" It further confirms that in the end times, the gospel will be proclaimed to all inhabitants of the earth. The "angel" that delivers this message may very well do so via internet transmission (screen name Gabrielxoxo?) Or maybe the "angel" he saw could have been a low-orbit satellite, visible at night like an airplane in the sky. Starlink uses low-orbit satellites. It seems time-consuming and conspicuous for one supernatural angel to literally fly around the globe and individually speak to billions of people. More logical and intuitive is that the internet itself, the global information superhighway, will be the key prophetic link to every human left on earth hearing the gospel of Jesus Christ. It enables audiovisuals proclaiming Jesus as Lord (through preachers, testimony, or “angels”), and it enables the written Word of the Bible to be available to all humans in all languages. So yes, I see worldwide access to the internet as a complete fulfillment of prophecy, or more accurately the vessel and practical means through which prophecy is fulfilled. These satellites can certainly be used for good if they are allowed to.

Technology has another key link to prophecy. We live in a world of 24-hour news cycles. Gone are the days where we exclusively get our world news updates at 6:30pm each weeknight from Walter Cronkite or Tom Brokaw. Instead, many of us live in a fast-paced world of information immediacy. In plain words, we hear about stuff real fast and from all over the globe. Growing up, I rarely heard about whether Japan was hit by a typhoon, or if a Pacific island had a volcanic eruption. But boy do we hear about it today and almost in real-time, and people share and react to this news through social media. Many of us have apps that give us breaking news alerts from around the globe. As I type in late summer 2023, wildfires have killed hundreds in Maui. Massive hurricanes are hitting regions they never hit, including California, Maine, Nova Scotia and the Mediterranean. Several thousand people have perished in the horrific floods in Libya from Hurricane Daniel. Thousands more have died from an earthquake in Morocco. Meanwhile, two dictators with nuclear capabilities are meeting in secrecy in Russia, one waging a war in Ukraine and one launching test missiles near his southern adversary. These are but a few examples of what I have “heard” about from news alerts on my phone this month. We hear of calamity on the regular these days. This itself is a fulfillment of Scripture. In Matthew 24:6-8, we read "You will hear of wars and rumors of wars...Such things must happen, but the end is still to come...There will be famines and earthquakes in various places. All these are the beginning of birth pains." Again, technology has allowed these prophecies to be fulfilled.

As a recap, the first event that will come to pass before the return of Jesus and the end of the world as we know it is the Rapture. This will inevitably lead to worldwide chaos and mark the beginning of the Tribulation, a period of extreme turmoil and suffering for those left on earth. The Man of Lawlessness will come into power as the sole world leader and reign for 3.5 years. He will have a right-hand man that helps him assume full dominion or facilitates and enables his reign (the two beasts of Revelation 13). Under the Beast, all will be forced to accept his mark in order to buy and sell food and goods. The Bible is clear that accepting the mark results in spiritual damnation (Revelation 14:9-10). Survival will be difficult without accepting the mark. Those who refuse will be persecuted.

In the spirit of "If it Happens, here's how it could", I feel the need to re-emphasize that the following is theory and theory alone. It is not Scripture. It is not a prophecy. It is not meant to add to or subtract from the Word of God in any way. It is one man's interpretations and analysis of Scripture and biblical prophecy and world events. Take it or leave it. Do not let it replace the gospel of Jesus Christ or the words of the Holy Bible. No man knows the day or hour of Jesus' return.

So how does the world change from what we know now, our everyday routines and 9-5 jobs and weekends watching football and dinner with friends and family and arguing on social media? How does the world as we know it change forever and lead to the

Great Tribulation? It seems certain a momentous event must occur to forever alter the trajectory of every human life on earth. This event will assuredly either be the Rapture itself, or it will coincide with the Rapture. Either way, **I believe the satellites orbiting our earth may be the key. These satellites are what enable much of the technological world we know today.**

Imagine if tomorrow, all the world's satellites were destroyed or went offline. What would happen? To be sure, all hell would break loose. As a society, we are dependent on technology, which is now largely dependent on satellites. That dependency grows with each year. Ten years ago in 2013, reporter Richard Hollingham of the BBC wrote a fascinating article entitled "What would happen if all satellites stopped working?" He had attended an international conference of experts regarding "space hazards." The threat posed by this scenario is chilling.

In this article, the first day of no working satellites is considered. The day begins with communication and entertainment inconveniences, such as the loss of tv signals and cell phone service. From there, things quickly escalate. Militaries lose contact with armed drones and with ships and aircraft around the world. Communication between world leaders and governments grinds to a halt. Air travel is stymied and grounded due to communication loss between pilots and air traffic control. Shipping vessels traversing the oceans are likewise cut off from the mainland. GPS enabled by satellites is lost. This affects more than Google Maps or your Garmin and extends into financial transactions and the internet at large, its complex existence reliant on the exact timestamps that GPS provides.

As the internet eventually goes offline, the infrastructure of our complex modern world would go offline as well. CNN and

Fox News and the rest would all be off the air. Power plants, water treatment facilities, nuclear reactors - all offline and their operations seriously challenged. Traffic lights would fail. The global supply chains for food, medicines, gasoline and goods would grind to a halt. Within a day or two, our homes, cities, the world would go dark figuratively and literally. Store shelves would quickly go empty. As the weeks went by, millions or even billions could realistically perish from starvation, dehydration, illness, conflict, or perhaps fires and explosions caused by riots and looting. It is unconscionable to consider the fate of abandoned nuclear facilities and power plants. The possibilities are endless but the danger is real. In 2020 at the start of the covid pandemic, we saw how quickly store shelves can empty and supply chains become compromised. Our seamless modern way of life can be stymied quicker than we think.

To reiterate, the fact is we as a society are completely reliant on technology. Most of us lack the skills of survivalists and settlers on tv shows like Naked and Afraid or even Little House on the Prairie. We are reliant on cell phones and the internet for communication and information. We are reliant on regional and global supply chains for most everything we conveniently get from stores - food, beverages, toilet paper, clothing, shoes, medicines, diapers, pet food, batteries, etc. We are reliant on electricity (refrigerators, ovens, microwaves, etc.) for food storage and preparation. We are reliant on technology to access our money and financial assets. Our modern technology, more than ever, is reliant on all those satellites orbiting up above. If anything ever happens to those satellites, we are in big trouble.

In September of 1859, the earth experienced the most intense geomagnetic storm ever definitively recorded. Known as the

Carrington Event (for astronomer Richard Carrington), this storm of solar flares caused auroral lights (Aurora Borealis in the northern hemisphere) to be seen around the globe, even near the equator. More importantly, it disrupted the primitive technology used on earth - telegraph stations. Telegraph operators around the world were electrically shocked and sparks flew. Beyond that, this intense geostorm was mostly harmless for the earth's inhabitants. There were no power grids and satellites to disrupt. People didn't lose electricity in their homes because they didn't have electricity. People went on with their daily lives. It was a simpler time. But this occurrence would have dire consequences for our modern world, something most of us have ignorantly never considered. Some scientists believe even more powerful solar storms than the Carrington Event have occurred in earth's past. One can internet search for the complex science behind this theory, as well as the science behind solar storms. Many scientists believe it inevitable that a geostorm with an intensity equal to or greater than the Carrington Event will befall the earth again. The consequences would be globally catastrophic.

Today as I write in 2023, ten years after that BBC article in 2013 imagining a day without satellites, the subject is again garnering headlines. You may have seen some in the news or on your social media feeds. Innocuous headlines like "Aurora borealis viewable in the continental US tonight" keep popping up. The science behind this, however, is not so benign. It turns out the sun is in a very active phase currently. Scientists are seeing a marked increase in solar flares and solar storms. The earth is increasingly being hit with weak geomagnetic storms. Many experts expect a peak in this solar activity in late 2024 or 2025.

As I write this chapter, the Wall Street Journal has just

released an article entitled "The Next Big Solar Storm Could Fry the Grid." It is chilling. Google it. Read this article. Journalist Christopher Mims opens with this: "One day, you wake up and the power is out. You try to get information on your phone, and you have no internet access. Gradually you discover millions of people across the U.S. are in the same situation - one that will bring months or years of rebuilding. A giant solar storm has hit the earth." The article details how vulnerable our technology is to solar storms. It is complicated physics. To summarize, the interaction of the sun's magnetic field (through fast-moving highly charged solar particles) with the earth's magnetic field can create powerful currents - currents that can knock out our electric grid and even the underground and under-ocean cables that are the backbone for our global internet. **Yes, scientists are sounding the alarm on a possible "internet apocalypse" befalling the entire world. But the effects are not limited to our infrastructure on earth.**

It turns out that the very satellites we rely on to maintain our modern technological world are indeed highly vulnerable to solar flares and geomagnetic storms. On February 4, 2022, the richest man in the world and SpaceX/Starlink launched 49 satellites into orbit. Within days, 40 of them had failed and burned up in the lower atmosphere, all due to a weak geomagnetic solar storm - exponentially weaker than the Carrington Event of 1859. This $50 million loss of Starlink satellites caused by solar flares is a chilling warning.

A year earlier, in a 2021 study and article entitled "Solar Superstorms: Planning for an Internet Apocalypse", University of California Irvine assistant professor Sangeetha Abdu Jyothi concluded that yes, earth's satellites are indeed highly vulnerable to solar storms. Should a high intensity coronal mass ejection (CME) befall the earth such as in 1859, it is conceivable and even likely that large numbers of satellites could be disabled or destroyed or thrown out of orbit, or at the very least their communication to earth (and therefore their functionality) disrupted for days, weeks, or even months. **Specifically, Jyothi estimates a 1.6% - 12% chance that a Carrington-level solar storm will strike the earth in the next decade.**

The first satellite Sputnik was launched in 1957, nine years after the rebirth of Israel into statehood. At the time of publishing, we are only 67 years into the existence of functional satellites. Scientists are only recently beginning to appreciate the threat and sound the alarm that satellites have not been fully conceived or engineered to withstand intense CMEs. To be sure, it is a ticking time bomb waiting to disrupt modern life on earth.

So what does this have to do with biblical prophecy? At any moment, a severely powerful solar storm could disrupt or wipe out our modern way of life. This could absolutely be how the Tribulation begins. But for those who believe in the Rapture, that is the event that begins the Tribulation. Could both events happen at the same time? Maybe so.

For faithful believers, God the Father, the Almighty creator of heaven and earth, is assuredly powerful enough to time this out. The Rapture could occur exactly when a massive CME strikes the earth. The faithful in Christ could immediately be whisked away from the earth, spared from the ensuing calamity and tribulation. Those left behind might not notice they were gone on a large scale, what with cell service and tv coverage all knocked offline. The Rapture could be explained away or overshadowed by the unprecedented geomagnetic solar storm and the earth descending into a primitive dark place. Without communication and information, the masses would not really know what happened and chaos and confusion and misinformation would be rampant.

But there is another possibility. It seems prudent to reiterate that the Rapture is most vividly described in 1 Thessalonians 4:17 and involves the dead in Christ and living Christians being caught up together in the air to meet the Lord. This seems like quite an event to happen "in the air", millions upon millions of bodies and souls meeting the Lord in our atmosphere. Instead of a violent solar geostorm, could this event itself knock out every satellite orbiting the earth? Could the brilliance of the Lord simulate an ultra-massive electromagnetic or solar storm that takes satellites off-line and renders most modern communication devices useless? Could millions of bodies and souls leaving the earth "in the air" (atmosphere) disrupt all those satellites? Could this event knock out only some satellites, leaving those in a different orbit unscathed? For non-believers, this likely sounds ridiculous. But for those of us who believe in the Rapture, is this possible? With God, anything is possible.

Going back to pure science, there is yet another very real threat to satellites. For years, more and more space experts have warned of "space junk." It is exactly what it sounds like, junk in space. More specifically, space junk is space debris (such as old or damaged non-operational satellites) that is either out of orbit or out of control. Not all space debris crashes back to earth or burns up in the lower atmosphere; rather, higher-orbit space junk continues to orbit the earth like new small moons. The problem is that space junk can interfere with functional satellites in orbit. Think of a satellite as a car on a large one-way circular highway miles and miles above the earth. Normally, its path is clear and it stays functional in orbit. But if a satellite encounters space junk, a collision can occur. This could have disastrous results, potentially destroying the functional satellite or knocking it out of orbit. The result is that now there is more space junk. Just like on a foggy interstate highway, a chain reaction could be set off. With more space junk, more collisions occur, creating more space junk, creating more collisions, etc etc. A catastrophic domino effect of satellite collisions could occur.

If this scenario sounds like a far-fetched cheap sci-fi horror flick, it isn't. Scientists are increasingly alarmed by the threat. Over the last decade, too many new players have entered the space arena, including private entities. It is not just one or two nations (like the USA and USSR from the last century) launching satellites. Several countries now have satellite launching capabilities, as do several private businesses. The result is that thousands upon thousands of new satellites are being launched every year by different entities. But nobody is launching more satellites than Starlink.

With each new launch, the likelihood of a space collision increases. A chain reaction of satellite collisions wouldn't happen instantaneously like a CME solar storm. Rather, it would be a drawn out event that should garner headlines and worldwide attention. Nevertheless, it is another very real possibility of how our modern technological world could be brought to its knees and set us back centuries. It also is an important way that only SOME satellites could be knocked offline. Many older satellites are in an upper atmosphere orbit around earth. Only more recently have low-earth satellites, including those of Starlink, become a reality. Imagine how much more vital and important those Starlink satellites would be if all other satellites in an upper earth orbit started colliding and failing. **Imagine if Starlink suddenly had a monopoly on communications satellites.**

If you watch the news or pay attention to world events, you may have heard a lot about Starlink recently. As mentioned, the goal of Starlink is to provide worldwide internet access via satellites, not landlines and cables that have enabled the internet for three decades. At the time of writing, Starlink is still a work in progress with new launches almost weekly, but its existence is already profoundly affecting the world at large.

In 2022, Russia invaded Ukraine, and war is still raging in late 2023 (as well as mid 2024 during this book's final edits). Much of Ukraine has been devastated in so many ways, including its technological infrastructure. Enter Starlink, which made relevant headlines in early 2023. It seems without traditional working internet access in some areas, the Ukrainian military forces became reliant on satellite internet access. A controversy ensued on whether the CEO would allow the Ukrainians to access his internet network. To his credit, he did. Still, the implications are unprecedented. **For the first time, astute observers saw firsthand how one un-elected billionaire in the 21st century could single-handedly make a real-time business decision to determine the fate of millions in a war-torn region.** Let that sink in.

The events in Israel and the Gaza Strip in the fall of 2023 left many shocked and saddened, but one headline in particular stopped me in my tracks. It seems once again, another war-torn region's militaries and civilians became reliant on Starlink for internet access. The infrastructure in Gaza is decimated, including the cables and wires that power the internet. Controversy again swirled over whether the CEO would allow access, and to which side or both or neither. This time, at the time of publishing, the stakes seem even higher and more consequential. This is a conflict in the Holy Land, the Middle East perhaps the most unstable and combustible region on earth. The threat of war contagion and a literal World War III is very real. The US has a nuclear sub in the region. The implications in terms of biblical prophecy have been explained. **Again, one un-elected billionaire with technical wifi wizardry has the ability to make the business and moral decisions that affect the entire situation. One man.**

Circling back to Revelation 6, recall that just before John sees the multitude in heaven, he writes of seeing stars falling to the earth. As mentioned previously, these cannot be actual stars that are massive like our sun. The earth itself would be destroyed if an actual star got too close, let alone fell onto the earth. So what did John actually see? What if all those "stars" descending from the heavens are satellites? These newer low orbit satellites are indeed visible to the naked eye for days after launch, like twinkling stars in the sky, only they move. If they or any satellites were to lose their orbit and fail, they could be seen falling towards the earth, perhaps in a fireball like a meteorite burning up in the atmosphere. Imagine thousands of satellites falling towards the earth at once. Is this what John saw just before or during the Rapture, or early on in the Tribulation? Did he see the satellites come crashing down and the world descending into chaos? Or did he see rockets and missiles of war? Either seems possible.

To be sure, if the earth's satellites failed, we would likely descend into millions of isolated primitive societies. Everyday would be a quest for survival. The world we knew would be gone, and in its place a post-apocalyptic society would emerge, the population eventually drastically reduced as only the strongest, smartest, or most ruthless survive. Food rations would be depleted, and those that survived would be reliant on rudimentary gardening and the earth's natural crops, vegetation, fruit, animals and fish. Modern farming (reliant on machines and mechanical irrigation) and shipments of food would be non-existent. Fresh drinking water too would be scarce or non-existent in many regions that are only habitable due to modern technology. Violent conflicts over supplies and rations would be commonplace. This nightmare scenario sounds alot like the plots of tv shows "The Walking Dead" or "The Last of Us." It also sounds a lot like the Tribulation as described in Revelation. **If society collapses, people will naturally look for a leader - someone to guide them, help them survive, fix the mess, get their lives back to normal.**

To summarize and spell it out as plainly as possible, I believe a disruption or destruction of the earth's satellites and electrical grids could be the beginning of the end. It could be the nexus event that will lead to earth's great Tribulation and the rise of a worldwide leader, the Man of Lawlessness. It is a highly possible and conceivable doomsday scenario that fits with the biblical description of both the Rapture and the Tribulation. Geomagnetic storms do not directly harm or kill humans like an asteroid strike or nuclear bomb would. Rather, a massive coronal mass ejection of solar flares (or the Rapture itself, or both) would leave un-raptured humans alive but alter their lives in every way. With the ensuing collapse of governments and society at large, the earth would be left reeling and with a power void. It sets the stage for one leader with his trusty tech genius ally to emerge worldwide, and again here's how it could absolutely happen.

Without satellites in orbit, worldwide communication would grind to a halt. Presidents and prime ministers and the like would have no immediate way to govern or maintain law and order. Their authority would be erased. Chaos would reign supreme. But try and imagine what would happen if a communication satellite or multiple satellites came back online or were somehow successfully launched. What if they were on the launch pad ready to go the very day and hour that the Rapture/geo-magnetic storm occurred, or at some point shortly thereafter. Or what if these select privately-owned non-governmental communication satellites, already in orbit, were spared, their lower orbit or technical advancements somehow enabling an escape from damage.

After days or weeks or months of despair and carnage, what would happen if worldwide communication and 21st century technology were slowly brought back online and restored? Would things just immediately go back to normal, the old world order restored too? Or would the person or people with the only functional satellites around earth hold all the power? Under this scenario, one or two people could indeed hold all the cards and become de facto gods. One or two beasts could emerge worldwide with a monopoly on 21st century satellite technology, a scenario more believable if one of those beasts is the current or former President of the United States.

It's time to correlate all this science and technology to Scripture. Recall the two beasts in Revelation 13. This book has focused on the leader Beast, the Man of Lawlessness. But what of this second beast? He is mentioned from verses 11-16. In verse 12, he "causeth the earth and them which dwell therein to worship the first beast." In verse 13, this second beast "doeth great wonders, so that he maketh fire come down from heaven on the earth in the sight of men." In verse 15, the second beast "had power to give life unto the image of the (first) beast, that the image of the (first) beast should both speak, and cause that as many as would not worship the image of the beast should be killed." In verse 16, we get to the mark of the Beast. But it is this second beast "which causeth all…to receive a mark on their right hand, or on their foreheads."

I am well-versed in contemporary commentary involving end-times prophecy, and this is where I diverge. The Bible describes the second beast as the "false prophet" (Revelation 19:20). A great deal of contemporary evangelical "experts" in this matter believe the second beast is therefore a highly religious man. They view his relevance in the passages of Revelation from the spiritual side, that he will be a spiritual leader. I do not.

I see the term "false prophet" a bit differently. I am looking for a man with worldwide fame and influence. He likely concerns himself with existential matters of human survival. He may be described as a revolutionary or innovator. Revelation assures us he will do great wonders and miracles (Revelation 19:20, Revelation 13:13-15). We are told he will specifically "maketh fire come down from heaven to the earth in the sight of men." I know of a man who does this. Commentators and theologians are looking for wizardry and magic, as if this second beast will literally conjure fire from his hand like a sorcerer or superhero. Think logically and practically. Do people already gather to watch fire ascend to the heavens and then fall back perfectly to earth? Do they applaud and marvel each time this occurs in Florida or California, each time a Falcon 9 rocket lands on a tiny barge with its tail of fire?

A false prophet inspires people into a new way of thinking, a way that involves humans not needing God. A false prophet gives a vision and hope for humanity to survive and endure forever, perhaps living even on other planets. A false prophet is only effective if they have a massive following and fan-base and infinite resources. When calamity befalls the earth (the Great Tribulation), the false prophet, along with the Man of Lawlessness, will be there to support and inspire humanity on their terms, in their way of thinking.

Think intuitively. Is it possible? One beast/titan emerges with the only source of satellite technology, those satellites already today being launched by rockets that appear as fire in the sky but land back on earth to cheering crowds (re-read verse 13 above and let think sink in). These satellites could be the only source of worldwide communication (with AI to translate into every language), the only means of getting the internet back online globally. Through re-establishing audiovisuals on the internet, this would fulfill verse 15 as "the power to give life unto the image of the beast" and causing that image to speak. That power sure sounds like the power of technology, and that image of the beast speaking sure sounds like videos and live feeds. How else would a man from 20 centuries ago like the apostle John describe modern-day videos? "Give life unto the image…cause the image to speak." The false prophet sounds exactly like a technological beast.

The end of verse 15 is sinister, insinuating that the second beast holds life and death in the balance at his whim. It is for the reader to decide if we are already witnessing that today in its infancy, as the fate of millions in war torn areas is being decided by the availability of satellite internet connectivity. Most assuredly, this technology could be further leveraged and weaponized if there is a monopoly and only one internet provider.

The passages in Revelation tell us that this false prophet will persuade mankind to worship the Beast. This will be done through the mark. The required mark of the Beast will show loyalty, but people will also be forced to accept the mark of the Beast to enable financial transactions. Otherwise, they will perish. In practical terms, if they can't buy food, they will starve to death. In this scenario, it follows then that the tech savvy false prophet and the Beast would be allies with a clear working relationship. For skeptics of this book, this will be an issue to keep an eye on. As I write in 2023, this may not be the case…yet. As I edit in July 2024, are two former adversaries suddenly becoming buddies?

And what of this one-world currency or means of purchasing goods during the Tribulation? Through his satellite wizardry, this second beast could also restore digital worldwide financial transactions. This is how he could be the person to enable this new singular monetary system worldwide. (He could even be a big proponent of this already - ever heard of cryptocurrency?) It follows that any enforcement of laws under the new authoritarian regime would utilize this man's internet technology as well. The other Beast - the Man of Lawlessness - would surely be an ally. He needs the second beast as described in the verses above. It may become a figurative marriage of convenience. The false prophet is the logistics man, in this case the technology man with infinite resources. With such an ally, the first Beast, the most famous man on earth, could sit perfectly poised to "save" mankind, poised to begin his worldwide reign.

It reminds one of "The Hunger Games", where all the technology-lacking districts have become subservient to one leader in the Capital, the Capital the only source of technology and communication to the rest of Panem. Former governments and leaders would be at the mercy of these two. Indeed, the entire world would be at their mercy. Is this how the most famous and ambitious and boastful public figure ever could rise to undisputed and uncontested power on a global scale? Is this how the richest, most tech-savvy man in the world could be by his side enabling it all? It is for the reader to decide if this seems absolutely outrageous or if it is fully credible and believable. **For the first time in any published book anywhere, this hypothetical fully explains a potential purpose and logistics of the second beast in striking detail as supported by Scripture.**

It is for the reader to decide how these men might react should the world lose satellite and internet connectivity. Does the above scenario seem far-fetched? Or does this seem exactly how they would react and capitalize on the situation as titans of business? Again, let the reader decide.

To be clear, the beasts of Revelation do not have to be devil worshippers or possessed or evil incarnate. They are not Satan. They are not demons. They are men. Whoever they are, it could very well be that they will just give in to their earthly desires (greed, power, or vanity perhaps), the very temptations Satan has enticed all men with since the Garden of Eden. Some say they may cause others to want the same things they want - lifestyles of the rich and the famous.

In this hypothetical which is not an accusation, it is for the reader to decide how the red-hatted politician would portray himself if he saved the world from an internet apocalypse. Some are asking if he would develop even more of a God complex. Does that seem about right, that upon orchestrating (or taking credit for) the restoration of technology and global communications and hints of normalcy for the masses, he could see himself as the literal savior of humanity? Could you imagine the proud boasts of unparalleled glory this man could declare he deserves from everyone on earth? Does it seem right on brand, or would he be humble and gracious? In this scenario, it seems natural people would gladly acquiesce, happy and relieved to be "saved" by an earthly leader. We have already heard how he believes he has done more for Christians and Jews than any man ever. How would he speak and act if he helped save humanity from certain doom? Would this enable a path to become a true worldwide authoritarian dictator? That is what the Man of Lawlessness will be, an authoritative dictator who demands absolute loyalty and worship. Demands absolute loyalty, does that sound like anyone in particular? Could you envision this expanding into a demand of worship as prophesied? It is all for the reader to decide.

Speaking of brands, this scenario again explains the singular worldwide monetary system during the Tribulation as described in Revelation 13. Recall that in order to buy and sell goods, all must accept the mark of the Beast, the name of the Beast or the Beast's number on his forehead or right hand. It does not take much imagination to see how this could play out. Upon restoring technology to the earth, the Beast and his sidekick could easily charm the masses worldwide. Great boasts and promises could be made. Vulnerable humans could be assured this new world order would just be temporary until all the satellites and technological infrastructure were back online and fully restored. In the interim, he could kindly and graciously reign supreme out of the goodness of his heart. Make the World Connected Again!

Banking systems and credit cards and all that would still be down, but not to fret. In conjunction with the false prophet who has the only working satellites, a new monetary system could be temporarily implemented. Perhaps it could be called MagaPay or just lowercase maga. Implantable microchips could be deployed worldwide, like uniform debit cards accepted everywhere complete with a maga tattoo on the hand. Perhaps he could employ less invasive smart watches worn above the right hand instead. Chips could even be sewn into hats already worn on the forehead. Might as well celebrate earth's new savior in style while shopping for food and goods.

Regardless of the specifics, some are asking - could you imagine anything more self-gratifying for the man who (some say) currently desires to have personally branded skyscrapers in every metropolis worldwide, the man who issues and sells his own fake currency to his devout followers? Could you see him demanding to build a skyscraper bearing his name in every major city around the world as a thank-you for re-establishing satellite connectivity? Could you envision him doing this in Jerusalem? Would that be the "desolation of abomination" as prophesied?

This wouldn't just be how a one-world monetary system could come to fruition, it is the clear-as-day why. It goes back to those deadly sins that the Beast, whoever he is, will so encapsulate, in this case greed and ego/vanity.

> Again, an edit to this chapter is in order. The global headlines keep leaving me speechless. It is beyond bizarre and unnerving to write about things, only to see them creep closer to actualization and fulfillment. In September of 2023, I was writing about a one-world uniform financial system that could come to pass if earth's current infrastructure was impaired. Fast-forward to early

> November 2023. It seems one prominent human is already working on making this a reality by the end of 2024! This story did not garner much attention at the time, so it is likely this is the first time you are hearing of it. So yes, perform your internet searches and read all about how one very wealthy entrepreneur already referenced above has grandiose plans to eliminate all banks (his words). In lieu of banks, you could use his super-app for all your financial needs! It won't just be for real-time communication anymore. It seems the previously secret plan for a worldwide monetary system on X (formerly Twitter) powered by the Starlink internet satellites is already in the works and ready to go live by the end of 2024. The far-fetched hypotheticals of this book seem to be happening in real-time and at a blistering pace. More and more pieces keep falling into place. Time is of the essence.

There are many possibilities as to how the Rapture and Great Tribulation could begin or play out. This chapter is just but one complex theory and not the only way. Only God Almighty knows all the details. But consider the above theory fully. Does it make scientific sense? Does it link up with Scripture? Could an internet apocalypse throw us into a chaotic time of literal tribulations?

Chapter 19 - What Now?

This book has posed many questions and presented many hypotheticals. The most prominent end-times prophecies from the Bible have been discussed and analyzed in the context of our modern world and current events. It is extremely unlikely that events will play out exactly as detailed in this book. This author is not psychic or a Nostradamus wannabe. This book is not prophecy and is not Scripture. Alas, it is just one man's take on how world events could be the fulfillment of prophecy. So what now? What should even a skeptical reader be looking for or doing?

First, continue to live your life. Live a life of goodness and love towards all people, friend or foe. Do not become so consumed by apocalyptic fears that it becomes an obsession. At the same time, maintain vigilance in terms of current events and biblical prophecy.

Second, this book has discussed the Rapture. It goes without saying that if millions of people worldwide just suddenly vanish one day - regardless of how it happens - that is a sure sign that the end is near. Do not be fooled or let anyone explain it away as normal. Do not believe a smooth-talking wolf in sheep's clothing.

Third, if our modern world descends into long-term utter chaos due to a worldwide technology collapse or internet apocalypse, raise your own figurative antenna ears up and take note. This feels like a sure way the Beast could rise to worldwide power.

Fourth, if one or two men do indeed rise up to "save" or rule the entire world, do not be fooled into following them in any way. This is clearly prophesied in Revelation 13. The Beast, aided by the false prophet, will one day come into full worldwide power. They are not saviors. They are doomed to destruction, as are any who follow them.

Lastly, if a single monetary currency becomes worldwide (and all other payment methods are eliminated), be alarmed. If it involves a required, mandatory mark or microchip or any payment method involving the right hand or forehead, do not do it. Do not take the mark. Repent and trust the Lord Jesus, regardless of the consequences.

Epilogue

If you have made it to the end of these pages, I wish to express my sincere thanks. This book has been an on-again-off-again project for two years, and it has been an extreme challenge to write.

First and foremost, I did not want this to be sacrilegious or unpleasing to the Lord in any way, nor is it meant to add to or take away from the Bible in any manner. The reader is encouraged to seek out the Word of God and let the Bible speak for itself.

Additionally, this potentially feels like a dangerous book to write should it actually garner any attention. A lot of soul-searching has gone into whether to publish. It is perhaps not the wisest decision to challenge and question two of the wealthiest and most powerful men on earth. They both tend to strike back when challenged. As such, there were several times I abandoned the project. But world events which seemed to eerily echo prophecy always drew me back in. As such, publishing this book is a leap of faith.

The preceding sections and chapters are all food for thought. The questions raised should not be interpreted as allegations. The discussion of current public figures should not be considered accusations. The analysis of world events in a prophetic context should not be misinterpreted as Biblical truth.

Ultimately, it is for the reader to decide if we could be living in the last days as depicted in the Bible. It is for the reader to decide if our high-tech modern world could be easily crippled should our complex computer systems fail or go offline. It is for the reader to decide if any Biblical depictions of the end of days seem to mirror current world events or figures.

As mentioned repeatedly, Biblical prophecy is hardly straightforward. The Scriptures are ancient writings that have been translated from their original texts. It is inevitable, then, that this book will be met with great skepticism. We live in the age of both thoughtful discourse and internet trolls.

This author welcomes skepticism. Never believe everything you read, including in this book. I exhort all readers to do their own research, to corroborate or fact check what is written in these pages. Read the Bible. Follow the news and current events. Think critically. Pray for wisdom and understanding. But maybe keep what you have read here in the back of your mind, just in case. And above all else, do not ever accept the mark of the Beast.

Bonus Chapter: The Curious Case of the Imaginary I.D.

This is your easter egg like in a Marvel movie, a bonus chapter at the end, a juicy little nugget. I couldn't ever find the right place to include it in this book's narrative. Anywhere it was included, it felt like it sidetracked things too much. Enjoy.

The red-hatted politician has been accused of stretching the truth or outright lying an infinite number of times. He has also been known to misspeak or get lost with his words during a speech. It happens. However, there is one bizarre, untrue claim that he has continued to pedal and mention at rallies and in interviews. Reporters and pundits and even his own allies are confused by his words. They don't know what he is talking about or what to make of it. Without evidence, he is claiming that "they" (the evil liberals?) are requiring citizens to show i.d. to purchase bread.

In the United States, identification (and age verification) is required to make certain purchases. The sale of things like alcohol, tobacco products, and guns have government-imposed age restrictions. These things are not that controversial - most people don't support the sale of liquor to third-graders, for example. However, nobody seems to have heard of identification being required to buy a loaf of bread. What is the red-hatted politician talking about?

The pundits and cable news analysts may be confused, but perhaps there is a real reason. This outlandish claim has very real apocalyptic roots. As mentioned repeatedly in this book, a worldwide authoritarian, the Beast, will come into full power during the Great Tribulation. Millions of evangelicals believe this. He will yield unprecedented global power over all of humanity. The Beast's mark will be required to purchase and sell ALL goods, not just age-restricted goods like alcohol. Yes, a mark or trademark will be required to buy a loaf of bread.

So why is the red-hatted politician fabricating this falsehood? Does he have dementia, or is there a purpose to the lie? Many assert that the red-hatted politician projects - that he accuses others of his own actions or crimes or shortcomings. Others claim that he repeats things often so that they take on a life and truth of their own, even if untrue. Still others assert that he gets out in front of an issue ahead of time, just in case. He claimed there would be voter fraud for months prior to the election. It ensured he couldn't lose. If he won by the numbers, it was fair and legitimate and required no challenges (as in 2016). If he lost by the numbers, it was only because of the alleged corruption and fraud. Heads I win, tails you lose.

Is that what is happening with the loaf of bread comments? Is he getting out in front of an issue before it is an actual issue? Does he know something we don't? Does he have a plan in the works to actually require identification or a mark to buy bread (and other goods)? Is this why it is being bizarrely mentioned repeatedly, to blur the lines on when it started and who started it? Whatever is going on, it has chilling echoes of Revelation chapter 13. Are we being primed for a coming military state where buying bread (or anything else) requires an approved mark or i.d.?

For further information and updates as world events merit, please visit:

www.gregorygatefield.com.

Made in the USA
Monee, IL
20 September 2024

66212258R00108